MODERN ARCHITECTURE

MODERN ARCHITECTURE

The Architecture of Democracy

REVISED EDITION

by Vincent Scully

GEORGE BRAZILLER · NEW YORK

For information, please address the publisher:
George Braziller, Inc.
171 Madison Avenue
New York, NY 10016

Library of Congress Catalog Card Number: 61-13689

ISBN 0-8076-0334-1

Printed in the United States of America

Sixteenth printing, September 2001

CONTENTS

Preface   *viii*

Preface to the Revised Edition   *ix*

Text

    Part 1: FRAGMENTATION AND CONTINUITY   *10*
    Part 2: ORDER AND ACT   *32*
    Part 3: TWELVE YEARS AFTER: *The Age of Irony*   *49*

Plates   *63*

Bibliographical Note   *135*

Notes   *137*

Index   *150*

Sources of Illustrations   *157*

"At this meridian of thought the rebel thus rejects divinity in order to share in the struggles and destiny of all men. We shall choose Ithaca, the faithful land, frugal and audacious thought, lucid action, and the generosity of the man who understands . . . . At this moment, when each of us must fit an arrow to his bow and enter the lists anew, to reconquer, within history and in spite of it, that which he owns already, the thin yield of his fields, the brief love of this earth, at this moment when at last a man is born, it is time to forsake our age and its adolescent furies. The bow bends; the wood complains. At the moment of supreme tension, there will leap into flight an unswerving arrow, a shaft that is inflexible and free."

—ALBERT CAMUS, *The Rebel*

"*Poet, patting more nonsense foamed*
From the sea, conceive for the courts
Of these academies, the diviner health
Disclosed in common forms. Set up
The rugged block, the image. Design
The touch. Fix quiet. Take the place
Of parents, lewdest of ancestors.
We are conceived in your conceits."

—WALLACE STEVENS, "*Prelude to Objects*," II

PREFACE

This book grew out of a talk, "Modern Architecture: Towards a Redefinition of Style," given in January, 1957, in Detroit, at the joint meeting of the College Art Association and the Society of Architectural Historians, and published as an article in Perspecta, The Yale Architectural Journal, *4, 1957, pp. 4–10; in* College Art Journal, *XVII, 2, 1958, pp. 140–59; and in* Reflections on Art, *edited by Susanne K. Langer, Baltimore, 1958, pp. 342–56. It has, however, been entirely rewritten, much expanded, and considerably rethought, so that I hope I have repeated myself as little as is consistent with the essentially unchanged historical view upon which the original talk was based. The text, therefore, does not pretend to present a full history of modern architecture, since much, including almost all city planning, had to be rigorously excluded from it, but it does attempt to define that architecture's historical dimensions, to evaluate its meaning in terms of modern life, and to trace the major developments which have taken place in it. The conclusions arising from such an essay can never be final ones. It is hoped, instead, that the illustrations as organized here, and the text as it relates to them, may suggest further perceptions and lines of thought in what is, after all, the unending attempt to define ourselves and our place in the world in which we, as modern men, are all engaged.*

viii *I am indebted to Miss Helen Chillman for typing and for much help in running down illustrations.*

PREFACE TO
THE REVISED EDITION

The reader is asked to regard the addition to the original text as an attempt to evaluate the major developments of the last decade or so rather than to cover or even to represent its architectural production regionally or by building type. To that end, many conspicuous monuments which do not seem to embody new or significant ideas have been left out—sometimes in favor, it must be said, of projects which will never be built. Unlike the earlier text, the addition includes as much city planning as could be crammed into it. The new captions put the architects' names first only because the old ones did. I apologize to the reader who, through no fault of his own, must cope here first with an Americanized version of existential idealism and then, all at once, with a rather sardonic empiricism not untouched by disillusionment and anger. A lot has happened in twelve years. But it should be pointed out that this approach requires, indeed permits, no fundamental change in analytical method, which remains a visual one. Architectural intentions and programs, in order to become—or in the case of drawings to move toward—architecture, have to result in physical forms, in which the human meaning is embodied and which, for those human beings who love them, remain a visual delight always.

I am still indebted to Helen Chillman.

1
FRAGMENTATION
AND CONTINUITY

"riverrun, past Eve and Adam's, from swerve of shore to bend of bay, brings us by a commodius vicus of recirculation back to Howth Castle and Environs."

—JAMES JOYCE, *Finnegans Wake*

Modern architecture is a product of Western civilization. It began to take shape during the later eighteenth century, with the democratic and industrial revolutions that formed the modern age. Like all architecture, it has attempted to create a special environment for human life and to image the thoughts and actions of human beings as they have wished to believe themselves to be. In these two fundamental attempts the modern man has faced psychic difficulties unparalleled in the West since the time of the breakup of Rome. The old, Christian, preindustrial, predemocratic way of life has progressively broken away around him so that he has come to stand in a place no human beings have ever quite occupied before. He has become at once a tiny atom in a vast sea of humanity and an individual who recognizes himself as being utterly alone. He has therefore vacillated between a frantic desire to find something comprehensible to belong to and an equally consuming passion to express his own individuality and to act on his own. Modern architecture has mirrored the tensions of this state of mind and has itself embodied the character of the age that produced them. It has acted as much more than a simple reflection of its society. Like all art, it has revealed some of the basic truths of the human condition and, again like all art, has played a part in changing and reforming that condition itself. From its first beginnings it has shown us to ourselves as modern men and told us what we are and want to be.

The "we," though dangerous methodologically for the historian, is necessary in speaking of modern architecture, as is the present tense, because it is an image we can recognize as ourselves that we must seek as we attempt to define the beginning of an art that is our own. First, we might travel backward in time until we reach a chronological point where we can no longer identify the architecture as an image of the modern world. This point

10

occurs, not at nineteen, or even eighteen, hundred, but about the middle of the eighteenth century. For example, the Spanish Stairs in Rome, of 1721–25, embody the character of the Baroque, not the Modern, age (plate 1). They create an active but totally controlled environment within an ancient European city. They are spacious and swelling and present an open invitation to the drama of movement. At the same time, their spaces, which seem so free, are in fact symmetrically focused by the solid shaft of the obelisk above them, behind which the church towers themselves can move for the pedestrian's eye. This may roughly be taken for an image of Late Baroque architecture as a whole. All movement is around fixed points. It is a union of the opposites of order and freedom. The order is absolutely firm, but against it an illusion of freedom is played. Secondly, for all the sculptural plasticity and humanistic imagery of the solids, it is in fact the space that governs the design, and the solids are entirely at the service of its dramatization.[1] It is therefore an architecture that is intended to enclose and shelter human beings in a psychic sense, to order them absolutely so that they can always find a known conclusion at the end of any journey, but finally to let them play at freedom and action all the while. Everything works out; the play seems tumultuous but nobody gets hurt and everybody wins. It is a paternal or, perhaps better, maternal architecture, and creates a world with which, today, only children, if they are lucky, could identify. This may be one reason why, since the Second World War, Baroque Rome has become a Mecca for some *literati* who would escape maturity, but it hardly makes Baroque architecture a kind of prototype of modern work, as some historians have attempted to do.[2] Instead, a vast gulf lies between it and such a modern monument as Le Corbusier's High Court for the government group at Chandigarh, the new capital of the Punjab (plate 2). In the latter, for example, the solids, not the space, have become dominant in the form. Thus the building, though helping to define a vast plaza, is also an isolated sculptural image, so designed as to be seen in relation to the profiles of the mountain masses to the north. The space between the natural and the man-made forms is essentially a void between opposing solids, so that the human beings who occupy it are neither sheltered nor brought to a single conclusion. Instead they are exposed to the two separate and hostile realities of human life: what nature is and what men want and do. In the Baroque, as at the Spanish Stairs or at Versailles, all, even nature, is controlled by the hu-

11

man will. At Chandigarh the human act in the building, itself harsher and more elemental than baroque opera could have imagined, is exposed to the reciprocal action of the natural world. A more tragic view of human fate than that held by the early eighteenth century prevails. The balance that results has the effect of a pact between antagonists. There is no outcome, no victory, only the splendid, precarious treaty and the blinding light of the recognition of what the realities are.

Yet Chandigarh is only one late result of a complicated process which began much earlier with the collapse, or explosion, of the Baroque world. That event was already prefigured before 1750, when Giovanni Battista Piranesi's *Carceri* etchings appeared (plate 3). Prophetically named, they were also prophetic in their forms. Though based upon the fantasies of earlier Baroque stage designs, and owing something to the asymmetries of the Rococo, they nevertheless projected a new image of violence at mass scale.[3] In them, the symmetry, hierarchy, climax, and emotional release of Baroque architectural space, like that of the Spanish Stairs, were cast aside in favor of a complicated spatial wandering, in which the objectives of the journey were not revealed and therefore could not be known. Men became small in a threatening environment of terrible masses, and that vertical element, the column, against which they had been accustomed to test their size and uprightness, now disappeared, while the arches swung in colliding orbits continuously from their chain-hung bases on the stairs.[4] It is already the end of the old, humanist, man-centered world with its fixed values—and the beginning of the mass age of modern history, with its huge environments and rushing continuities.

Many architects of the early nineteenth century and later understood the new character of Piranesi's vision. Some of Sir John Soane's interiors for the Bank of England, for example (plate 4), seem almost directly derived from it, as do the interiors of his own house. The arches spring fluidly from the walls without the interruption of entablatures; light filters in from unexpected places; the vistas go on mysteriously with no apparent conclusion. But it is the modern engineer—wholly released by his nineteenth-century materialism and positivism from the humanist tradition—who has, on his own terms, constructed Piranesi's world at its appropriate scale. Paxton's Crystal Palace of 1851 overthrew the old stabilities of mass and compression, and the skeleton structure of thin iron members was seen by his contemporaries as a delightful maze (plate 5). It was a place to wander in, endlessly continuous, with only glassy boundaries and with the solids fragmented into complicated webs. The Eiffel Tower, built for the French exhibition of 1889, celebrated similar compulsions and has become the landmark of modern Paris, but the Galerie des Machines (plate 6) at the same exhibition, found the most appropriate program, as its three-hinged steel arches swung continuously from the pavement to house vast batteries of machines and crowds of tiny human beings: Henry Adams' Dynamo and its worshipers.[5] In Max Berg's splendid structure of reinforced concrete, the Centennial Hall at Breslau, of 1913 (plate 7), the arches loomed upward in a twisting curve, creating the appropriate environment for mass political man. Violent continuity and the smallness of the individual were, here again, its themes. In the Livestock Pavilion at Raleigh, North Carolina, of 1953 (plate 8), the roof is suspended in tension from continuous, intersecting arches, leaping out and away from the edges of vision like Piranesi's arches themselves. In all these ways the old stabilities have been overset, and human beings, in the mass, have been given an architectural environment which is an image of the modern world itself, in which they do not know exactly who or where they are.

We should note that the forms created by the engineers cannot have arisen simply because new materials became available, as some critics would have us believe. Rather, the formal and iconographic framework for them pre-existed, as the work of Piranesi and Soane shows. The common recognition has been that of continuity as an engrossing fact. Conversely, an engineer like Nervi may react against that recognition to insist not only upon a precasting system that makes a structure of small-scaled, separate pieces of concrete, recalling the coffering of the Pantheon, but also upon a return, by choice, to the pure circle, with central oculus, of the Pantheon itself (plate 9). At the same time Nervi's engineer's instinct makes it impossible for him to reinstate the vertical column in a domed structure, so that the slanting profile of his slab is continued by that of its supporting piers. On the other hand, the desire to reject continuity is as old as its first appearance at the beginning of the modern age. Indeed, the consciously revolutionary architects of the later eighteenth century most emphatically embodied that desire. The eye of Ledoux wished to look out upon a space no less vast than Piranesi's but, unlike the latter's, spare, static, and Spartan, like that of the equally revolutionary paintings by David (plate 10). Instantly, the order which the Baroque had masked in play was swept clean of its old grace notes and presented as a stark fact at mass scale. Thus, Ledoux's project for a Salle de Spectacles, of 1778, may be seen as the direct ancestor of the Reichs Congress Hall at Nuremberg, of 1936 (plate 11). Here, the columns do not disappear; instead they are made endlessly repetitive. Men themselves are arranged as massive architectural blocks. Isolated stands the leader, Robespierre or Hitler, to whom they give themselves body and soul in order to escape the fearful loneliness of an uprooted social system and who fills the void left by the disappearance of God.

One result, therefore, of the collapse of the Baroque synthesis of freedom and order was the fragmentation of that synthesis into its separate components. It is perfectly logical that this should have occurred, since the end of the old directed world left each man free to exploit his own particular powers, predilections, and limitations to the full. Out of that fragmentation the two movements which may loosely be called "Romantic-Classicism" and "Romantic-Naturalism" took form.[6] Each was romantic because it focused with exaggerated emotional intensity upon a single, restricted aspect of human experience. The former concentrated upon the creation of clear geometric order (plate 13). Its forms had none of the rhythmic invitation of the Baroque, nor were they primarily spatial but, instead, sculpturally separate and solid. They were intellectually precise and sought an ideal, timeless abstraction, believed by their creators to have been characteristic of antique, sometimes Roman, but more particularly Greek, architecture. The earliest publications of that architecture during the eighteenth century do in fact embody the hard, linear quality of a frozen ideal (plate 12). The plastic action of Greek temples was not perceived at all, nor was their relation to the natural world. It was not action that was wanted, but perfection.[7] Again, the Romantic-Classic attitude, as formulated by the first architects of modern times, can be traced from them to the present, linking together Stuart and Revett, Ledoux (plate 13), Jefferson (plate 14), and the early work of Le Corbusier (plate 15), where, however, as will be discussed later, it began to be enlivened by essential elements it had lacked before.[8]

The countermovement to Romantic-Classicism was Romantic-Naturalism, its exact opposite and contemporary. If the former may be described as the art of the revolutionary, the second is the reflex of the refugee, the art of the suburbs. It insisted upon freedom and upon an escape from the harsh rigor of the intellect into a world of intuition and "natural" values. It avoided the fixed climax of the Baroque and the symmetry that was normally common to Romantic-Classicism and the Baroque alike. Its forms were not linear and planar like those of Romantic-Classicism but coloristic and painterly, i.e., "picturesque." Its asymmetrical planning and massing, its use of rustic materials, and its suburban orientation, may all be traced from long before Marie Antoinette's *Hameau*, of 1782 (plate 16), to the present. In this development the projects of the English landscape architects of the later eighteenth and early nineteenth centuries and of the Americans of the mid-nineteenth played a significant part, as did the "natural" suburbs based upon them and the light, highly articulated wooden houses with which they were furnished. The American "Stick Style" houses of c. 1840–76 (plate 17), the work of Greene and Greene in California during the early twentieth century, and that of their followers of the present time (plate 18) are all products of this "romantic-naturalist" mode.[9]

The fragmentation of the Baroque synthesis of opposites was thus complete by the early nineteenth century. Since the meanings of hierarchy and control upon which Baroque architecture had been based no longer existed, and since a tradition which essentially ran all the way back to Rome had been permanently interrupted, upon what foundation of purpose could a new synthesis be attempted? The answer which most critics have proposed for that question, so far as the middle of the nineteenth century is concerned, involves the two concepts of "Eclecticism" and the "Picturesque," and demands a certain extension of the meaning of the second term beyond that used above.[10] That is, since the spatial (environmental) and sculptural (active) qualities of the old forms per se were now devoid of specific meanings, they could be chosen as seemed appropriate and rearranged as desired. Since this "eclectic" method was purely one of optical titillation, having nothing intrinsic to do with the program or structure of a building, but producing a great variety of effects, it partook of the pictorial freedom of painting and was thus doubly "picturesque." This was true even of Victorian Gothic design, however desperately iconological, "realistic," and structural it tried to be.[11] Therefore, even the harsh forms created by architects such as Butterfield (plate 20), who demanded, like the Ecclesiological Society, which was his sponsor, that a building should embody Christian "truth" and "reality," or by Viollet-le-Duc, who based his architectural theory almost entirely upon a system of structural determinism, reflected the general picturesque sensibility.[12] A process of developing combinations consequently took place throughout the period. This process curiously re-enacted the entire course of western architecture and finally managed to work its way back to a kind of pseudo-baroque design, drained of emotional focus and of meanings other than theatrical ones, which became the stock in trade of architectural schools by the end of the century. The Provincial Baroque, "Georgian" manner of the great mass of building in England and America during the first half of the twentieth century was characteristic of this last, persistently catatonic phase. The process can be followed (plates 19–22), from the "Valhalla" at Regensburg (Parthenon on Praeneste) to All Saints' Margaret Street (Ecclesiological Gothic) to the Louvre of Napoleon III (Medieval and Renaissance) to the Paris Opera (Beaux-Arts Baroque). In the end, it is almost as if the democratic and industrial revolutions had never taken place. At the same time the common picturesque, nineteenth-century method of all these buildings ensures that they can hardly be mistaken for the products of any of the ages they invoke, while, strangely, the interiors of some of them, most particularly of the Opera, might almost have been designed by Piranesi.

We are therefore led to the question: In what, beyond the evasive action of "choices," did the nineteenth century truly believe? The answer, as we can read it from nineteenth-century philosophy, science, and historical writing, would seem to be that it believed in continuous movement, in the process of evolutionary change itself.[13] This was a measure both of its confidence in the future and of its separation from the fixed values of the past. We have already noted, in Piranesi and in the work of the engineers, that such continuity was imaged at the beginning of the modern period and remained a dominant motif in some of its most characteristic forms thereafter. At the same time, a reading of nineteenth-century thought also indicates that the period—like all ages that are rent—believed in polarities of human experience, in oppositions, as between the forms of Romantic-Classicism and Romantic-Naturalism, or between what it itself called "Classic" and "Romantic" modes. We have seen that the mid-century attempted to combine those modes through selec-

16

tive recombinations of older styles but that the productions of such "Picturesque Eclecticism" came to double back upon themselves rather than to move forward—which, as we have noted, it was apparently the nineteenth century's most earnest wish to do. It is therefore not surprising that the period's rather schizophrenic polarities could eventually be resolved only in terms of what was most naturally pervasive in its view of life, that is, in terms of continuity. And since, of all the cultural divisions of Western civilization, America was the one to which the future seemed most open and in which the sense of actual uprootedness was most strong, it was in America that the polarities were first swept away in terms of a new, continuous architectural order.

It is clear that the European in America never felt entirely fixed in place upon the continent. He had left the closed garden of the European landscape behind him, and his new natural environment was larger, more hostile, and above all, less bounded than any he had known before. The American was therefore the first European to experience the continuous flux of modern times, and his most characteristic literature, from Cooper and Melville to Whitman and Twain, celebrated images of homelessness, movement, and continuous flow.[14] Those images were pervasive by the middle of the nineteenth century. A popular print of 1868, struck just before the golden spike which linked East and West was driven into the railroad ties, shows the American's sense of the vastness of the place, of the impermanence of human habitation upon it, and of the call of Whitman's "Open Road" across it (plate 23). The Brooklyn Bridge, of 1867–83, was seen in another contemporary print as a glorification of that road, not so much linking places as leaving them and shooting on untrammeled across the open sky (plate 24). Similarly, the most characteristically American buildings of the colonial period, however closely imitative of European prototypes they may have been intended to be, were usually thin screens around interior spaces, light and impermanent, with their Provincial Baroque details dwindled into the linear pattern of a drawn curtain.[15] They both sealed themselves against the place and gave the impression that they might at any moment be swept away by it. Jefferson had consciously wished to express the permanence of the new republic with his more solid romantic-classic forms (plate 14), but these too had always looked hauntingly adrift upon the vast land. Then, during the middle of the century, the American house, partly inspired by Gothic Revival theory, literally jumped out of its skin, expressed its structural skeleton, and projected itself outward in bays and porches (plate 17). This was the "Stick Style," flexible and active but still embodying in its own way another expression of utter impermanence.[16]

It was Henry Hobson Richardson who first brought the inherent American instinct toward continuity into union with the equally inherent and constantly growing desire for permanence and security. His Watts Sherman House, of 1874, smoothed over the mid-century expression of the skeleton (plate 25). It stretched the late medieval-early Renaissance elements of contemporary English work into horizontally extended window screens, cutting through the big gable that sought to contain them. By the early eighties Richardson and many other architects had transformed influences from early American colonial architecture itself (plate 43) into thin, shingled skins of wall, tightly stretched by the pressure of the continuously open spaces inside them and engulfing the exterior spaces of porches into their volumes[17] (plate 26). Continuity and permanent shelter were thus united as a single theme. That union of opposites was even more striking in Richardson's masonry architecture. His Ames Gate Lodge (plate 27) makes a cyclopean statement of human permanence on the American earth, even of an autochthonous heroic age upon it, but the mass of the building stretches out on the horizontal, and its great arch swings, like the arches of Piranesi (plate 3), from the ground. The power of Richardson's forms gave a demonstration of unmatched confidence to those architects who most closely followed and understood him, and that confidence was in three things: in continuity, in permanence, and in the power of a building to embody an heroic attitude. Richardson's Marshall Field Warehouse in Chicago, of 1885–87, shows all these qualities best (plate 28). It assumes position with the massive authority of a Renaissance *palazzo*, but its arches stretch vertically upward, while the horizontal spandrels slide tightly behind them so that the whole surface dilates with the pressure of the vast horizontal open spaces it contains.

Louis Sullivan, perceiving the quality of the Marshall Field Warehouse, described it in anthropocentric terms: "Here is a man for you to look at. A man that walks on two legs instead of four, has active muscles . . . lives and breathes . . . in a world of barren pettiness, a male. . . ."[18] Sullivan then used this building as the fundamental inspiration for his own mature design. In his Walker Warehouse, of 1888–89 (plate 29), he stretched the arches all the way up to the attic floor and recessed the spandrels somewhat, so that the exterior became a plait of articulated three-dimensional members rather than a taut screen. Then, in the Wainwright Building of 1890–91, his first great skyscraper, where the masonry elements were merely the cladding over a steel skeleton, Sullivan abandoned Richardson's arches, doubled the vertical piers, and inserted the whole plait of piers and spandrels into the frame created by base, attic, and corner planes (plate 30). Note should be taken of the fact that every other pier has no structural column within it, and that Sullivan was therefore consciously stressing both the verticality and the plastic density of the building and avoiding any expression of the structural bay—upon which the other architects of the Chicago School, with their "Chicago" windows, were all concentrating (plate 31). Sullivan's intention was more complex and humane than theirs. The form that "followed" the function for him was not that of an open steel cage but that of a physical force, contained but vertically standing. Finally, the Guaranty Building, of 1895, brought all the elements together (plate 32). The building now really stands on its columnar legs, but these are contained by the corner frames, which both define the volume and hold it down, stretched upward as they are to the cornice. There the static slab of the Wainwright Building is abandoned, and Richardson's arches reappear, but the thin piers that they connect seem to be not so much rising up to them as pulling down like a dropped screen within the larger frame. A drama of vertical continuity, hung weights, and human uprightness is realized at once by the observer's empathetic association of himself with the visual analogies for compression and tension that Sullivan—even in the ornamental surface—manipulates so skillfully; the building seems to stretch and stir "walks on two legs . . . lives and breathes." Sullivan is still unique among American architects in his desire and ability to develop this empathetic analogy; in his time he was unique among Americans and Europeans alike. He was the great, perhaps the only, humanist architect of the late nineteenth century, as he brought into the mass metropolis—in terms of its new program of the skyscraper office building—a dignified image of human potency and force. But the concept of "empathy" was itself a contemporary one and was proposed as central to the architectural experience by Geoffrey Scott, in his book, *The Architecture of Humanism*, of 1914.[19] In these terms, Sullivan was capable of making a human analogy, even a human image,

19

out of the principle of vertical continuity itself, appropriately applied to a free-standing, mid-space, and thus potentially active building. In his Carson-Pirie-Scott Store of 1899–1904, Sullivan created a complementary, space-bounding type, capable of defining a street or a square (plate 33). Here, consequently, the body image was abandoned. The surface is horizontally continuous, except at the corner, where it splits apart as if under interior pressure. The columns are kept back in plane, and the horizontal "Chicago" window is used, while the light-splintering ornament of the lower floors takes all sense of structural support away from that zone. The upper stories are therefore floated free of attachment to the ground and released for the velocity of their movement down the street, and for the down-shifted, controlled slide of their turn at the corner.

The horizontal continuity of the Carson-Pirie-Scott Store, and even its "floated" upper stories, were characteristic of many American Shingle Style houses of the eighteen-eighties (plates 34–35a). These were the suburban equivalent of Sullivan's urban invention, and they also derived from the impetus given by Richardson's design. Out of them Frank Lloyd Wright's early work directly grew, to culminate, integrate, and, in one sense, to complete the American nineteenth-century development as a whole.[20] The origins and character of Wright's design cannot be discussed in detail here. But the main point which should be made is that it was overwhelmingly spatial in intention and effect, not, like Sullivan's, humanistically sculptural. In it the open, horizontally extended plans of the eighties were stabilized at their centers by fireplace masses like those of American colonial houses, while the crossed axes of space—a type of plan also used in the eighties[21] (plate 35a)—were carried continuously outward to porches and terraces (plates 36, 37). The whole fabric was integrated around this spatial idea, so that the building broke out of the old containing skin to enhance the continuity of its space and to embody it plastically both inside and out. "In my work," said Wright, "the idea of plasticity may now be seen as the element of continuity." Or again, "Here . . . principle . . . entered into buildings as the new aesthetic, continuity," and he claimed to have discovered "the new reality that is *space* instead of matter," and to have created, in this way, "The Architecture of Democracy"—in which claim, as our earlier discussion of "continuity" would indicate, he was not far wrong.[22] While the spatial dominance in his work may in one way recall that of the Baroque, Wright's was a space compulsively expansive and flowing (plate 40), like Whitman's Democratic Open Road or Twain's River, not humanistically fixed, and he threw out the essential element of the old humanist design. "Have no posts, no columns," he wrote. Even the influences upon him in plan and structure from the American tradition of frame construction (plate 17) and from Japanese architecture itself—as from the Ho-O-Den at the Chicago World's Fair of 1893—were transformed by him through the elimination of all posts at the corners (plate 37).

The constantly fluid spatial quality of Wright's design can be seen even in those masonry houses which were most heavy, solemn, and densely massed, but whose separated, interweaving planes of wall should be contrasted with Richardson's engrossing shells. In this way Wright was able to unite continuous space with a new kind of monumental mass, permanent and earth-evoking, expressing, not a sculptural act, but rather its wholly spatial purpose which fulfilled itself in the compelling environment it created. This was equally true of Wright's larger, even his vertical, buildings as well, which were often closed off from the outside and lighted from above. Thus, in the Larkin Building, of 1904 (plates 38, 39), the interior volume is created by an interwoven structure of columns and spandrels, with vertical service towers at the corners. All these elements are fully revealed upon the exterior, so that the whole is much more integrated in space, structure, and massing than any building by Sullivan. Nevertheless, for all their abstract power, its solids become—and were intended to become—simply an expression of the interwoven and contained spaces they made, not an analogy for the standing human body, as Sullivan's had been (plates 30, 32). Wright's spaces themselves were not intended to celebrate or encourage the human act but to mesmerize the individual through the total unity of the environment in which he was placed (plate 40). Therefore, ideally, the furniture of Wright's houses was built in, scaled to the architecture, not to the human use of it, and the spaces were not only continuous but also low and dark, like those of early colonial houses (plate 43), thus finally achieving full expression of the opposed American impulses toward movement and security. So, in the Robie House, of 1908–09, the massive chimney of colonial tradition now holds the building down, as the very low, compulsively extended horizontals of the living spaces burst out of the traditional box and seek to take wing

21

(plate 41). The old solid order of things—still felt in the weight of the building—is fragmented into its components, and these are rearranged into the shifting patterns of a continuous movement through space (plate 42). In this way fragmentation, one of the essential elements of meaning we discover at the very beginning of the modern age, was given precise formal definition and united with continuity in the architecture of Wright's first maturity, as it also was in the contemporary Cubist painting of Europe.[23]

The period beginning roughly in 1914 marks a decisive break in Wright's career and, it would now appear, in American culture as a whole. Its peculiarly nineteenth-century invention seems to have played itself out, so that the historian must turn back to Europe in order to trace the development of modern architecture further into the twentieth century. There again the last great nineteenth-century images are of continuity. One might almost be tempted to regard the architecture of *Art Nouveau* as an ultimate phase of the Picturesque-Eclectic process, moving beyond the Baroque to the Rococo, so that an interior by Victor Horta (plate 44) seems almost the same kind of weightless, curvilinear bower as does a room in the Hôtel de Soubise. But *Art Nouveau* certainly derived from many sources—all of them nonclassic, like the Celtic interlaces beloved by William Morris, which may also have played a part in forming Sullivan's rather similar ornament.[24] Its curves were not nervous and teasingly interrupted like those of the Rococo, but continuously fluid, snaky, and submarine. Horta's interiors create an environment of flux and becoming, a Bergsonian world which embodies the endless continuities that move through all things, including man, and in which all separateness drowns (plate 45). It seems an appropriate conclusion to the scientifically confident and evolutionary nineteenth century, and it recalls the intuitions of the first philosopher-scientists of Western civilization: the Ionians, who embraced the concept of physical continuity and who, with Thales, saw water as its essential element. In the Maison du Peuple, with Herakleitos, we cannot "step twice into the same rivers, for other and yet other waters are ever flowing on."[25] Ionian philosophical thought may have owed a good deal to the Minoan ritual tradition, as we can read it in Minoan art, where everything celebrates the fluidly unilinear movement of nature and all its creatures (plate 46). It can hardly be coincidental that Minoan art itself was being excavated and published from the last third of the nineteenth century onward, and that Evans' free-wheeling re-

22

constructions at Knossos were as much *Art Nouveau* as Minoan.[26]

Something deep thus moves through *Art Nouveau*; it was more than a decorative (or decadent) style, as some historians would have it be and as those who destroyed it claimed. It seems especially profound when its influence touches Antonio Gaudi, to whom continuous structure had indeed always been sympathetic.[27] The Casa Mila, both in plan and elevation, is like a sea-hollowed cliff, its rock-cut façade water-smoothed and eroded, hung with metal seaweed and dug with windows like eyes (plate 47). The whole "rolls round," like Wordsworth's early-nineteenth-century image or a late painting by Van Gogh (plate 48). It seems to embody a total human participation in the rhythms that infuse the natural world. This is why the strange gods that crowd the roof of Gaudi's sea-formed acropolis enjoy such an eerie life (plate 49). They come, as icons and guardsmen, from somewhere underneath—hollow, plated, and helmeted—and take their places above and beside the broken stairs. This is also why Gaudi's is a convincingly Expressionist architecture, in its own way a forerunner of Surrealist sculpture and painting (like that of Picasso, another Catalan), and why later "Expressionist" buildings, like Mendelsohn's Einstein Tower, tend to be less convincing (plate 50). The latter is mechanically streamlined but is not moving and therefore means nothing, but Gaudi's forms, like those of the best of *Art Nouveau* as a whole, are infused with the action of nature and are therefore somehow real.

The imagist method of *Art Nouveau* can never have been fully applied to more than a comparatively few buildings. Before 1910 a strong reaction against it was under way, on grounds which were not only rationalistic and to a certain extent classicizing but which sought to reject the principle of continuity as well. One part of the new movement was embodied in the work of Auguste Perret, who claimed a rigid technological determinism for his work in concrete. Yet Perret's buildings, from 1903 onward (plate 51), totally avoided any expression of the continuous oneness of part with part which all poured-concrete structures actually have, and which Max Berg's Centennial Hall at Breslau so beautifully demonstrated[28] (plate 7). Continuity of form is so natural to concrete that most historians, before Gaudi's Casa Mila was adequately published, casually assumed it to have been constructed of that material. Perret's rejection of continuity was therefore largely an arbitrary one, based upon his fondness for the discontinuous frames of medieval carpentry, which he imbibed from Viollet-le-Duc, and for the rectangular bay system, with paneled infilling, of French seventeenth-century classicizing design (plate 51). It is true that form work is simpler for a rectangular skeleton, and that rather statically designed solid or perforated panels can be easily precast and set within the frame. This was done in the Church of Notre Dame at Le Raincy, of 1923, perhaps Perret's finest building (plate 52). Here, too, the curved slabs of the canopy are so adjusted to each other that the columns take what are essentially only point loads, as in a trabeation system, and the whole becomes a simple, static pavilion of space. Doggedly combining its Victorian Gothic structural determinism with its classicizing, not romantic-classic, formal predilections, Perret's design looked rather better to most critics a few years ago—when, as will be discussed later, the most recent revival of the regularly expressed bay system and of classicizing order took place—than it had looked in the thirties. Yet, despite its solid qualities, and as it can be seen in the large at Perret's extensive reconstruction of Le Havre (plate 53), it is so inhumanly inert, so intellectually and emotionally arid, and in some ways claims so little for architecture, that its influence is clearly waning at the present time.

The revolt against *Art Nouveau* which took place in the German countries at the beginning of the twentieth century was more complex and eventually more fruitful. It too was based upon a kind of rationalism and upon certain classicizing, perhaps here more truly romantic-classic, predilections. Otto Wagner's Post Office, in Vienna, of 1904–06 (plate 54), should be contrasted with Horta's Maison du Peuple (plate 45). The linearity is now taut and hard, and the individual elements, despite the curve of the ceiling, are essentially rectangular and seek a machined, not an organic, character. The design has been swept clean of movement, of overt continuities, and of what the period itself would have called "decoration." In that sense it recalls Ledoux's Spartan reaction against the Rococo, to which I earlier compared *Art Nouveau* itself. The obsessive puritanism of the Austrian reaction was summed up in the contemporary polemics of Adolf Loos, who equated "Ornament" with "Crime" and categorically attributed sexual perversion to those who employed it.[29] Loos' own design of the period carries further the stripped, linear, taut, and planar character we saw in Wagner's (plate 55). In all this it is as if the revolution of more than a hundred years before were being re-enacted and its harshly abstract principles reaffirmed. The new European forms of the beginning of the twentieth century were thus generally to express a separateness between men and nature and to embody a sense of the hard clarity of human experience. These ideas were counter to Wright's evolutionary continuities and his mesmeric space, though they were eventually to be affected by both.

The potential of the revolution in Germany was realized and given solidity because of the presence of Peter Behrens, a great builder and teacher. Behrens' work itself indicates that he felt a link with the early Romantic-Classic architects, especially with Schinkel. His Turbine Factory, of 1909 (plate 56), combines the awesomely scaled geometry of romantic-classic form with the new—I think, equally romantic—dramatization of machined materials. (It should perhaps be pointed out that no Romanticism of the Machine had appeared in the forms of Richardson, Sullivan, and Wright. Despite, or because of, the fact that America was more completely than Europe the very child of the machine age, the machine has actually played a minor role in American emotional life, and the impulse to dramatize it for itself has been extremely rare. It is normally disguised as something else.) The steel bents of the Turbine Factory are exposed at the sides, and their profile makes the shape of the massive gable, beneath which the masonry walls, scored in huge courses, batter deeply inward and from which a taut curtain of metal and glass is (visually) hung. It is a design of pure power, and its combination of Romantic-Classicism and the Romanticism of the Machine underlies the form of the Fagus Factory, of 1910–14, by Walter Gropius, who was one of Behrens' many excellent students. At the same time, the Fagus Factory is less potent but perhaps more fully integrated than Behrens' work (plate 57). A curious resolution between structural logic, continuity, and classic preferences keeps the columns back from the corner but sheathes it tightly in glass all the same. Certain interior details of the Fagus Factory indicate that Gropius might have received some influence from the work of British architects published in Germany, such as Voysey and Mackintosh, and perhaps even from Frank Lloyd Wright (plate 58). The latter was published in Berlin by Wasmuth, in two volumes, in 1910 and 1911. Gropius' reaction to these seems to have been almost instantaneous. The façade block of his Model Factory at Cologne, of 1914, clearly derives from Wright's Mason City National Bank, of 1909,

25

published by Wasmuth, and may also be related to the similarly published Yahara Boat Club Project of 1902[30] (plates 59, 60). Yet Gropius was obviously being torn two ways. He was impressed by Wright's continuously horizontal planes, but he wished to avoid his deeply spatial plasticity of mass and desired, in a very European way, to bound and close the building's profiles. Thus, he encased his own building in a skin—on the court side of glass, on the other of rather neoclassic masonry with distended glass stair towers erupting like bubble gum from the corners (plate 61). Gropius' design during the rest of the teens and the early twenties further documents his dilemma. He wanted a kind of continuity and an expression of spatial movement lacking in Behrens, but he wanted it in closed, hard, romantic-classic, and machined terms. How to resolve the paradox?

The answer to this question, critical as it was for the formation of the International Style of the twenties, was worked out by those Dutch architects, sculptors, and painters who generally took part in the movement called *de Stijl* and out of whose work the principles of "Neo-Plasticism" and "Constructivism" took form.[31] Here again the influence of Wright must be affirmed. Other Dutch architects copied his work almost exactly, but *de Stijl*, despite the debt that movement also owed to French Cubist painting, took it and transformed it. Taking a view of the Willitts House, of 1902, as published by Wasmuth (plate 62), we may concentrate upon the linear pattern and derive a Van Doesburg of 1918 (plate 63), and more remotely a Mondriaan, from it. Ignoring the lines and focusing upon the advancing and receding volumes, we may derive a "construction" by Vantongerloo, of 1921 (plate 64). Taking the process a step further and reading the planes as forming hollow, interlocked boxes, we may arrive at a Neo-Plastic house project by Rietveld and Van Doesburg, of 1920 (plate 65). Going only one step beyond this and separating some of the planes further, we can come to Rietveld's demonstration, of 1924 (plate 66). In all the cases so far considered, a linear and planar clarity of separate parts has been combined with continuously shifting sets of spatial relationships. Next, if we take all these experiments and smooth them out to a single plane—combining strict linear and rectangular order with the flux and movement of calculated asymmetries, as Mondriaan had done by this time—we arrive at Oud's Café de Unie, of 1925 (plate 67). Finally, join all the planes firmly into boxes and interlock their separate volumes into an asymmetrical composition like the continuous but mechanical movement of a set of gears, and it is Gropius' Bauhaus, of 1925–26, that emerges (plate 68). Note should be taken that the strong lines of Wright and the early Van Doesburg have all disappeared and have turned into edges, so that there is no expression of a structural frame, but only of thin, perforated sheets of stuccoed wall surface (plate 69). Shifting patterns of movement, eventually derived from the continuities of Wright, had now been combined with romantic-classicism's geometric separateness and abstraction and with a machined sharpness and angularity as well (plate 70). This synthesis, or compromise, formed the International Style of the twenties and thirties as it was understood by most of its practitioners. It is unfortunate that some of the bolder spatial experiments of earlier neoplasticism were not constructed before the rather academic adjustment was affected, but at this moment (1960) their potentialities seem, as published, to be of considerable interest to architects once more.[32]

The most spatial design in Germany during the twenties was that done by Mies van der Rohe. His work of that period also documents the contest between American and European sensibilities, which has been referred to above, and it achieved the most illuminating synthesis between them.[33] Mies was also a pupil of Behrens, and his project for the Bismarck Monument, of 1912, was pure romantic-classicism, a great masonry machine. After the war he was touched by influences that would seem to have come both from American skyscrapers and from constructivist sculpture in transparent materials, like that of Naum Gabo (plate 71). In 1923, his project for a Brick Country House took the long, continuous cross axes of Wright and interrupted them rhythmically in ways which recall the paintings of Van Doesburg (plates 72, 37, 63). In elevation (plate 73), the project was a romantic-classic and neo-plastic organization of interlocked cubes, attempting to stabilize, with their masses, the long horizontal continuities of the space. Other houses by Mies of the twenties also show this attempt to reconcile the American compulsion toward movement with the European instinct for closed, bounded forms. In the German Pavilion at Barcelona, of 1929, Mies was able to bring the opposites into harmony with each other. The building sits upon a platform, almost a classic podium, but one that is mounted from the side (plates 74, 75). The columns and slab of the structure are clearly separate from the asymmetrically placed planes of wall that lead the observer in a

27

fluid, asymmetrical movement through space. But the road is contained on both ends of the platform by closed wall planes, recalling those of a European garden, which enclose two pools, like bounding seas. The building itself recalled the gleamingly machined, environmental and therefore not figurally active, forms of the constructivist sculptors. It was thus purely spatial, its solids thinned and dispersed, but in the smaller pool stood the figure of a woman by Kolbe, balanced on a rock and gesturing with her outstretched arms (plate 76). Toward this image the observer was led, seeing it first through the black glass, "darkly," and then coming out to it where its act was exposed to the sky and framed by the constructivist planes. Now, however, its sudden, precarious gesture seemed to be creating the constructivist environment around itself and, once seen, controlled the building completely. All the planes seemed to be deriving from it, positioned by it, even as its lifted arm could still be faintly perceived from the far end of the platform (plate 77). Consequently, the union was optimistic and exact: mobility and enclosure were reconciled; the architecture of a precise but fluid environment was shown as created by the human act. The Barcelona Pavilion was thus the temple, perhaps appropriately temporary, of the International Style, and it embodied the ideal symbols of the European and American components which had gone into its creation.

Mies' strength lay in his willingness to work only with the ideal. It was also his limitation. If he was forced to compromise—as at the Tugendhat House, of 1930 (plate 78), in which a fluid plan had to be partly encased within a box—the result was not entirely satisfactory to him. Because of this, Mies' design moved during the thirties toward the more perfect enclosure of the court, where the open plan could remain free inside, and toward a more classicizing symmetry of space and massing. But his opportunities to create the ideal were limited in Europe, and Mies was not able to construct his final vision of an almost Platonic perfection until he found a sympathetic ambient for it in the architecturally hopeful but sadly confused America of 1939. In order to understand what occurred there after that time it is first necessary to consider the later phases of Frank Lloyd Wright's design.

Perhaps the primary fact of Wright's career after 1914 is that he had already outlived the nineteenth-century culture which had produced him and whose myths he had so completely embodied.

28

He was therefore alone. One might say that the mobility of American society has similarly isolated the creative American of every generation, which is one reason why it has been so difficult for American artists to mature. This was especially true at the moment of passage, about 1914, between two very different Americas, the old one with a few roots in the earth, tough and inventive, the new one fully industrialized, purse-proud and insecure. Wright's inventive contemporaries in Chicago and California were effectively finished by the shift: Purcell and Elmslie, Greene and Greene, Maybeck, Gill. Wright refused to be. He fled, in space to Japan, in time to the pre-Columbian civilizations of Central America and Mexico. His problem was to find and express what was permanent, and, like so many modern men, he looked for the answer in the forms of non-European society, outside the Hellenic and humanist traditions. He was not looking for an image of the human body or the human act. Instead he sought the images of nature's permanence, and he found them in the monumental weight of Mayan architecture, in the compacted mountain shapes of its pyramidal temple bases and the mansarded profiles of its concrete temple masses.[34] The Barnsdall House, of 1920, is an excellent example of Wright's use of such forms, here imitated partly in poured concrete, partly in stuccoed frame construction (plate 79). By 1923, however, Wright was able to integrate his desire for Mayan mass and richness of surface mosaic with a structural system of reinforced concrete blocks, and many projects of the twenties further demonstrated his capacity to think through the Indian shapes in terms of new uses and structural systems. The St. Marks Tower Project, of 1929, was one of the loveliest of these, an integral kind of tree growing out of the earth (plate 80), a point-marker in space, not a space-dominating image of human force like Sullivan's Guaranty Building (plate 32). Curiously, the skyscrapers of New York, built during the twenties by the well-armored rear guard of Beaux-Arts architects, had also turned away from Sullivan's types toward an imagery of road and mountain not so different from Wright's at this period. Some were towers, the Open Road turned upward, because the objective was simply to keep going, higher than anyone else had gone, if possible. Others, under the impact of new zoning laws, studied the possibilities of "set back" masses, based, as Hugh Ferriss' rather frightening drawings of the period show us, upon a study of mountain forms, and resembling, when finished, a Mayan temple base egregiously exploded in scale.[35] Thus the foreign visitor to New York may see, at the very edge of the continent and crowded insanely and splendidly together, the forms which were the two opposing symbols of life in America—the white and the red, the road and the mountain—all floating, appropriately enough, upon the water (plate 81).

By the thirties Wright was able to grow into a second maturity and to create a new synthesis in his design, because he now had something equivalent to test it against, that is, the developed work of the Europeans whom he himself had influenced almost a generation before. There can be no doubt that masterpieces like "Falling Water" (plate 82) represent the third phase of the International process, in which Wright welded together almost everything that had gone before: his early work and its continuous space with Mayan pyramidal massing, structural continuity in reinforced concrete with neo-plasticism, the thin, machined screen of metal and glass with the asymmetry and nature-worship of romantic-naturalism and the geometric clarity of romantic-classic form. He did much the same in his smaller "Usonian" houses, the units for his "Broadacre City," disciplining his Jeffersonian desire for life on the land with new structural and heating techniques and with elements in space and planar composition both his own and Mies' (plates 83, 77). He therefore found the partners for an essential architectural conversation, such as he had not enjoyed for more than twenty years. It is unfortunate that the conversation was not able to develop into a truly intellectual give-and-take on both sides. With the exception of Mies, who freely acknowledged his debt to Wright (and, of course, of Richard Neutra, who had worked with Wright in the twenties and whose own design was another synthesis between Wright and Europe), the Europeans who came to America, especially those around Gropius, refused to accept Wright as a modern man and regarded his work with condescension, despite the influence it had exerted on their master in his early days. Most serious of all, they passed this attitude on to most of the excellent students who now flocked to them. Wright responded vigorously and not always wisely, so that he remained bitterly alone. Therefore, surrounded by an almost feudal court of hypnotized apprentices and disciples, he wrapped himself up in the cloak of the pioneer and followed the old Open Road forward with ever increasing velocity. At Taliesin West he found the ideal spot for the culmination of his lonely American myth: the empty desert, beyond Cooper's "sea of trees" and "sea of grass." There he was able to pile up his concrete masses, like the dance platforms of Teotihuacan, and to spread his canvas planes above them, like the tent of the nomad or the hood of the Conestoga wagon (plate 84). In plan the space is again a dry river (plate 85). It flows through the building in long "reflex" diagonals, to reveal, at the loggia, the pure emptiness of the desert and to focus, on a direct cross axis, upon the mountain which rises behind it (plate 88). Now the road is the labyrinth, "dancing the mountain" upon the desert's face. Note should again be taken, not only that such exact orientation of a processional axis through a spread-out building upon a solid mountain form is universal in Cretan art, as I have indicated before,[36] but that Wright's architectural masses here, though eminently plastic, are still conceived as space-defining, like those of Crete. Similarly, their profiles compact the mountain's shape; they do not complement it with a contrasting but equally sculptural image of the human presence. Instead they avoid reference to the human body and abstract the natural environment in their forms. Taliesin West is therefore not a Hellenic exploration of the tragic balance between man and nature but a simple recognition by man of nature's engrossing power and a ceremonial submission of himself to it. Conversely, like all Wright's work in the landscape, Taliesin West draws the landscape forms themselves into the shifting patterns of human emotion by its very echoing of them. They are thus involved in the romantic "pathetic fallacy," by becoming images of what men feel, rather than separate, stable facts on their own.

Significantly, at this moment in time, Wright's circular forms began, recalling those of *Art Nouveau*, which had themselves been evocative of Crete. But Wright's were more spatially compulsive. At the Johnson Wax Building, they pulled the observer inside their non-bearing, and thus purely space-enclosing, walls, through the low portal, to the great high room inside with its lily-pad columns—these, too, reminiscent of Cretan forms (plates 87, 88). The images are still of the road and the river, but now they have been made to lead to an interior hollow of perfect engulfment and peace, a true Calypso's cavern of relaxation and security. This was the "Great Peace" Wright constantly referred to in the lectures of his last years. I have elsewhere attempted to show how these forms, and their meaning for Wright, closely related to Roman architecture and its Mediterranean prototypes

31

as well, and it is certainly clear that Wright's plan for Florida Southern College was closely derived from the plan of Hadrian's Villa at Tivoli.[37] It is the interior space, maternally rounded and swelling, that counts in both, and the exterior is primarily an expression of that hollow volume inside. So at the end of his life Wright recalled his beginnings and, in a sense, the whole road he had traveled thereafter. The Morris Store sends the road up in a continuous spiral—like the labyrinthine symbols carved in the neolithic earth sanctuaries in the shape of the goddess on Malta—and closes it off entirely from the outside world within an arched shell of wall that recalls Richardson's forms (plate 89, 27). In the Guggenheim Museum the time-defeating spiral makes the exterior shape balloon outward, and the continuous concrete surface is given its weight-destroying coat of paint so that "space, not matter," may become the whole "reality" (plate 90). Lighted from above and wholly enclosed, the Guggenheim Museum once more embodies the two opposites of perfect security and continuous movement (plate 91). It is wholly the expression of a wish-fulfilling environment, in which everything flows together and no individual act is possible or necessary. As such it is the final monument to the mobile, mass-moving aspect of American democratic mythology, and it brings the spatially continuous phase of modern architecture, inherent since Piranesi, to its only possible denouement and, probably, its close.

2   ORDER AND ACT

"A new Ulysses leaves once more Calypso for his native shore."

—PERCY BYSSHE SHELLEY, *Hellas*

The dilemma implicit in the later stages of the continuous phase can be seen in the Harvard Graduate Center (plate 92). Here the rectangular buildings lost the harsh clarity Gropius' design had embodied in the twenties and were pulled into a continuous, asymmetrically fluid relationship which was counter to their intrinsic nature—as the tentative connections between them show so well. The old International Style compromise was breaking up; continuity no longer worked, and everything was vitiated by the attempt to retain it in forms inappropriate to it.

Bauhaus philosophy was incapable of resolving this new dilemma, since a serious lack of relationship had always existed between its sociological pretensions and the abstract process (*De Stijl*) through which its design had actually developed. Into this situation Mies van der Rohe brought an uncomplicated intellectual order and a wholly integrated design. His early classicism now came into its own at the Illinois Institute of Technology, where he kept the buildings separate from each other, defined both mass and void by a single module, and allowed what continuity there was to expand naturally from a symmetrically conceived central space (plates 93, 94, 95). The nineteenth-century compulsion toward movement was finally cast aside. Now the Renaissance townscape was recalled, conceived as it too had been upon a modular system of fixed perspectives. Instantly everything settled down. Asymmetry and flow had been exorcised, and all buildings brought into simple, cubical volumes. Therefore their fabric itself could be studied with a new kind of care, since it was no longer simply a matter of planes defining spaces. The fixed, classical skeleton of the rectangular frame, now of steel members with brick panels set between them, could be expressed once more and its intersections reverently elaborated. Mies' work thus took modern architecture out of the suburb and off the road and set it down in the center of the city once more.[38] Its link with the humanist traditions of the Renaissance (which had always been venomously disliked by Gropius and Wright alike on social grounds derived from the weirder aspects of Gothic Revival theory) was instantly recognized in both England and the United States (plate 94). The relationship was made clear by Peter and Alison Smithson's Secondary School at Hunstanton, England, of 1951–53 (plate 96). Here the planning, massing, and detailing show the influence of Mies, and the general symmetry was further suggested, so Smithson has said, by Rudolf Wittkower's contemporary book, *Architectural Principles in the Age of Humanism*, which was largely a study of Renaissance proportional systems.[39]

Mies' later work and its influence thus tended toward the reduction of asymmetry and of spatially fluid forms, and a re-

33

newed concentration upon the building as an ideal fabric and an expression of humanistic order. Ideally, Mies would have only one cool, static pavilion for all functions, as his Farnsworth House shows (plate 97). The pavilion was to be defined by a structural frame, eventually dominated by the vertical column in steel. In the Lakeshore Apartments, Mies expressed the columns on the exterior and also welded vertical metal I-beams to the frame, forward of columns and mullions alike (plate 98). Thus, as in Sullivan's work, the vertical unity of the building was stressed. These devices integrated the skyscraper as a vertically standing object, in a way that the simple expression of the structural bay, clad by the icy American screen wall, could never do, and as a total suppression of the skeleton in favor of a complete glass and plastic curtain could hardly accomplish either (plate 99). On the other hand, the vertical unity of the Lakeshore Apartments was partly vitiated—in comparison with Sullivan's Guaranty Building, for example (plate 32)—by the projection of the column. This caused the structural and spatial bay, horizontal in proportion and expressive of a cage rather than of a sculptural body, to be read through the vertical elements which sought to conceal it. In his Commonwealth Apartments and his Seagram Building Mies solved that problem by keeping the columns back in plane and by designing the spandrels in elegant panels, as Sullivan had done (plates 100, 101). This allowed the vertical I-beams to dominate the exterior, so that the Seagram Building can stand upon its legs, symmetrically placed behind its plaza, as a sculptural body, not a structural cage or a spatial hollow. In this way Sullivan's image of human uprightness was returned to the center of the city, though now in Mies' rather frozen, thin, classicizing, and essentially inactive form.[40]

Mies' importance in America after 1950 arose from the fact that he brought with him a decent, teachable way of building, which had enough of the old humanist, urban character about it for it to be appropriately used in the city, where it was most needed. His classicizing limitation of himself to a few simple shapes, to "almost nothing," was at first a virtue but it had certain dangerous restrictions in it, since it answered all problems by ignoring most. The dignity of his high, single spaces, the statement of a perfect environment which did not compel men to movement, or mesmerize them, but left them alone, can be seen in his Crown Hall for the Illinois Institute of Technology, his Project for a National Theater in Mannheim (plate 102), and his Cullinan Wing for the Museum of Fine Arts in Houston (plate 103). The structure is kept outside the space so that nothing disturbs the interior volume, and the whole fabric, especially at Houston, expands gently with a relaxed and classical command. Mies' lucidity and calm thus seemed to offer the perfect solution in design for a generation that was confused, rather tired, and sick of complication, sociological argument, and mobility alike. It was not a romantic-classic solution but a classicizing one, evoking in steel a premodern, total order which recalled that of Perret's in concrete but was more subtle and sensitive than Perret's had been. It offered noble detachment, with all the disengagement from struggle implicit in that state of being.

Mies' civilized dignity was best understood by Philip Johnson, who became the foremost spokesman for the new classicizing design and, beginning with his own house at New Canaan, of 1949, an important architect of it in his own right (plate 103a): Even Johnson's most recent buildings thus essentially derive from Mies, although the influence of more specifically romantic-classic modes can also be seen in them. Both his Museum for Utica and his first Project for a Theater of the Dance for Lincoln Square, in New York (plates 104, 105), recall the revolutionary projects of Ledoux and Boullée, but they also have the taut, stretched, and rather nervous quality which we saw to be characteristic of American work of the pre-Richardsonian period. This point will be returned to again; what is significant at the moment is the conscious historicism of Johnson's method, seeking as it does to reverse the clearly outworn process of spatial continuity and to recapture the clarity of the first architectural intuitions of the modern age. Thus the exterior of Johnson's Synagogue for Portchester, New York (plate 106), of contrasting geometric shapes, most decidedly recalls both Ledoux and the eighteenth-century publications of Greek architecture (plates 12, 13), while its plan and its hung vaults (plates 107, 108) reveal the influence of Rome, again most particularly of Hadrian's Villa at Tivoli. The building is more of a shell or container than Mies' somehow more expansive structures are, and the tightness and thinness of its forms—as, for example, in the vaults—can also be matched in American colonial practice. This quality of thin container has been shared by many of Eero Saarinen's buildings, in a personal series based at first upon Mies. The planes of his General Motors Research Center are stretched into membranes, as are both the dome slab and the glazing of his Auditorium for

M.I.T. (plate 109). The latter again reveals the neoclassic formal method, which is to force all functions, appropriately or not, into a single geometric shape. Again recalling Tivoli, and Wright as well, Saarinen's Chapel for M.I.T. is a hollow shell of brick standing in a pool, lighted from above and below, so that the play of light upon the water is reflected on the undulating wall inside. Both Johnson and Saarinen thus developed toward a kind of design which was usually romantic-classic but which, in whatever idiom tended toward rather arbitrary eclecticism and impatient formalism.[41] At the same time, both of them—along with other architects, such as Rudolph and Johansen, who have moved through the classicizing phase and out of it—now seem to be consciously searching for some method whereby their work may be liberated and enriched.

The necessity for finding such a method has been amply demonstrated by recent developments in America and elsewhere. The neoclassic reduction of all buildings to single pavilions for all functions has had, as one might have expected, the good effect of making it possible for untalented men to produce bearable designs, but it has had the bad effect of causing better architects to concentrate upon the superficial decoration and embellishment of the pavilion, rather than upon more profound problems of function and structure.[42] Stone's grilles, behind which anything can be hidden, are an example of this, as is his rather feminine scale (plate 110). In Yamasaki's recent work the impulse to embellish the neoclassic cube has actually led to the fragmentation of its mass into a nervously linear pattern of precast concrete components. At Wayne University and elsewhere, these even split the building up the middle into a kind of twittering aviary (plate 111). All these developments document once again the age-old tendency of American architecture to become thin and decoratively linear, especially when based upon prototypes which are, like Mies' work, not only urbane and European but also essentially linear themselves. Most characteristic of all is the thin, icily gleaming screen wall, endlessly repetitive and expressive of that utter separation from the place which we saw to be characteristic of America's earliest works[43] (plate 112). Richardson and Wright had broken up such Puritan fleshlessness, but with the dwindling of Wright's influence after 1950 it has most emphatically returned as the ultimate expression of bureaucratic design.

The new classicism has been most pervasive in America, al-

36

though its reverberations have been felt throughout the world, creating a period of rest, or of reassessment, in the general development of architecture. The question which most architects were asking by 1960 was how they could free themselves from its restrictive vise without a return to the old, compulsively continuous design or to the unsatisfactory compromises of the International Style; how, at the same time, they could use both the function and structure of a building to create its form more directly and to give it more plastic solidity than the International Style, with all its talk of function and structure, had ever cared to do. Structural exhibitionism of the "space-frame" or "geodesic" (Buckminster Fuller) varieties—though still prevalent and involved, like neoclassicism itself, with single spaces—was hardly the answer, except for special wide-span programs, since the problem of functional accommodation, for human activity is normally too complex to be legitimately solved or architecturally developed in so simple a manner. Therefore, the answers which have seemed to offer themselves have all been involved with the concept of human action. The work of Alvar Aalto, as it has progressively liberated itself from the International Style, is a case in point.[44] Aalto's buildings, especially those of the past twenty years, have all seemed to grow out of a direct response to the kind of human action they were intended to provide for. They do not embody such action in a figural sense, but they contain, encourage, and dramatize it, and their shapes seem to derive from it. Thus the plan and section of Aalto's church at Vuoksenniska (plate 113) should be contrasted with both those of Johnson's Synagogue and Wright's Guggenheim Museum (plate 107). The Johnson plan is of separate static shapes, the Wright of a demandingly repetitive geometry. Each is in its own way an inflexible imposition upon what goes on inside it. But the entire Aalto plan, and the section as well, seems to billow outward along radii that derive from the preacher's voice at the altar. The shell of the building responds to the sound within it and wraps its planes flexibly around it (plate 114), giving with it—while its tower suddenly shoots up to explode above the pines, marking the spot where, below, the voice is sounding (plate 115). Similarly, in Aalto's housing project for Munkkiniemi (plate 116), radial sight lines, recalling the effect of many archaic and classic Greek temene, control the placement of the building masses, responding to each other and to the site as they take position in space: batted out, as it were, by the pliant main slab.

37

Precisely because he sends the eye from one building to another, and past them to the landscape across irregular spatial intervals —because, that is, there is no spatial module—Aalto stresses the fact that the building solids, not the spatial voids, are the positives in the design. Space, again as in archaic and classic Greek temene, is simply what is left over between them. The masses are not controlled and dominated by the modular order of the void; they themselves control and dominate the void. Therefore, paradoxically enough, the space is freed, but, most important, the solids are released to act, as, for example, those at Harvard and I.I.T. alike are not (plates 92, 93). Aalto's method is therefore at once functional, visual, plastic, and flexibly expressive. In his civic center for the town of Säynätsalo, one thinks of Romantic-Naturalism among the pines, where the forms are hard, the profiles jagged (plates 117, 118). But the brick masses cantilever out above the lower zones with a threatening instability and dramatize entrance into the court along the stairs between them. The building solids are so arranged as to invite such movement and to respond to it, and the cutting edge of the high council chamber, with its linked joints gathered inside it like clasped hands, rises above the other profiles as the appropriate termination of a climactic shape around which all the other masses move.

Aalto's design is convincing because, unlike the new classicism, it is interested in what people do and, unlike Wright's work, does not attempt to smooth out individual actions into a single rhythmic movement. On the other hand, it is still partly picturesque, because the structure is pushed around at will for the complicated compositional effects desired. The next step, therefore, has been one that has sought to integrate what the building is to be used for with a structural system that is not only necessary to the function and the form, but that also makes its own active demands felt, or, as Louis I. Kahn puts it, "What does the building want to be?"[45] Or, more specifically, how do the spaces that the functions require want to be made? Kahn's answer, beginning to take shape with the Yale Art Gallery, of 1953, and gaining strength with his project for a Community Center at Trenton, of 1956–59, first involved a rehabilitation of the column or pier as an integrally space-defining solid. In this way Kahn was able to go beyond classicism's line and plane to a columned bay system three-dimensionally conceived, like Brunelleschi's, but more archaic in its mass. At Trenton (plate 119), each grouping of low or high columns, making both major and "service" spaces, had its own precast concrete roof cap, so that the building would have created an elaborate environment of separate but densely grouped structural entities, seemingly capable of standing, crouching, withdrawing, advancing, like a whole Birnam Wood on the march. Finally, Kahn's Medical and Biology Laboratories for the University of Pennsylvania integrate space and massing with structure, through a system of concrete columns, crossed beams, and spandrels (plates 120–122). Thus the setting created for human action does not seem an arbitrary extension of the human desire for utterly untrammeled perfection—as those by Mies do—but has a challenging, rational, and solemnly active reality of its own. The topological sequence of the structure, which creates the cantilevered bays of the exterior, embodies an intellectually exact pattern, while the brick-clad towers, more simply powerful than anything by Aalto, house stairs and exhaust- and intake-vents for the laboratories. Their vertical masses recall the noble, actively grouped, compellingly urban towers of those medieval towns, such as San Gimignano, which Kahn no less than Aalto loved; but they, too, are "what the building wants," vertical circulation and breath. Kahn's method in the Medical Laboratories is therefore perhaps closest to Wright's in the Larkin Building (plates 38, 39)—a structurally "organic" method—but Kahn avoids Wright's engrossing envelope and his euphoric spatial interweaving. Instead, here as in later projects not yet complete, Kahn's design enforces human recognition of an environment both meticulously realistic and heroic in itself: one which is intended to make the scientist feel not in command but both mysteriously and comprehensively challenged. So Kahn's buildings are reverently built, monumentally constructed of toughly jointed parts. They reject the easier releases of spatial continuity and neo-classicism alike, and most architects seem to regard the method which is producing them as the most potentially creative, truly "objective," one in use today. The movement carried on by the "Brutalists" in England, most particularly by Smithson, is symptomatic of the trend: first toward Mies, then toward Aalto, now in the direction of Kahn. James Stirling's and Colin Wilson's work, while showing the same trend, seems most directly influenced by some of Le Corbusier's later buildings in brick and concrete,[46] but the achievement of Le Corbusier has been so unique in modern times that it deserves to be discussed in conclusion and on its own.

39

Le Corbusier has been the most influential architect of the past forty years.[47] I should like to consider only a single aspect of his work, but one which seems to me to be the most important and, perhaps, the least understood.[48] It is this: Le Corbusier, after a lifetime of consistent effort, finally discovered a means for embodying the human act in architectural form, almost as Sullivan had done, but more passionately and, if I may use the only other appropriate term, more ironically. That is to say, Aalto's architecture, as we have seen, derives from human action and expresses itself as a flexible container of it and, in group designs, as an equilibrium between active masses, while in Kahn's the environment for action becomes a kind of integrated, demanding force itself. With Le Corbusier the case is different. His method became one which made a building not only a container for human beings and their functions—as most buildings are—but also—as most buildings are not—a sculptural unity that itself seems to act, like figural sculpture, and so acting to embody the peculiarly human meaning of the function it contains. In accomplishing this, Le Corbusier has created the monumental architecture of his time, even while his colleagues of the C.I.A.M. (International Congresses of Modern Architecture) were debating whether or not monumental architecture was a "good" thing, or about the need for it, or about how it would come when society was finally "integrated." Le Corbusier's is a modern monumentality because, like all monumental art, it deals with the most naked revelation of what the best of our thought believes to be real, which—so most metaphysical philosophy of the mid-twentieth century would indicate—is not the City of God, or the state, or afterlife, or a political dialectic, or material progress (which has never produced a monumental art yet), or even ourselves, but only our acts as we acknowledge them, try to understand them, and, if possible, to ennoble them.[49] Yet in the broadest sense, the human act is balanced by the natural world and its law, which is separate from the human self and with which man carries on a reciprocal communication and a finally hopeless contest all his life. For the architect the landscape stands for the whole of the natural world; and it is in harmony with and in contrast to the particular landscapes in which they are placed that Le Corbusier's most recent buildings are designed to act. Such reciprocal action between opposites is Hellenic—with the proviso that the Greek temple was conceived not as a purely human gesture in the landscape but as the body of a god who, however, was himself the embodiment of a certain kind of potential action or state of being that men could recognize as real and important in terms of the facts of life as they could be known.[50]

Le Corbusier thus did what the first, late eighteenth-century, revolutionary seekers after the plain truth of things in Greece had failed to do. He perceived that Greek temples were compact and active sculptural forces, the opposite of the purely receptive hollow of the Minoan palace, and that their abstract forms were meant to be seen in a complementary relationship with the counterfacts of the natural landscape. He perceived this at the very beginning of his career when, after having received his initial impetus from Behrens, Perret, Berlage, and others, he set out in search of his own spiritual past. His journey was not to an exotic culture, but to the Mediterranean and, most specifically, to the Acropolis of Athens, where men, a little like modern men, had first become exposed and free (plate 123). There he saw what no archaeologist had so clearly stated before, that the axis around which the temples acted was controlled by the distant landscape forms. "The axis of the Acropolis," he wrote in his *Vers une Architecture*, of 1923, "runs . . . from the sea to the mountain." He went on: "The Greeks on the Acropolis set up temples which are animated by a single thought, drawing around them the desolate landscape and gathering it into the composition."[51] He said of the Maiden's Parthenon: "This creates a fact as reasonable to our understanding as the fact 'sea' or the fact 'mountain.'" And of the Propylaia leading toward it: ". . . nothing . . . left but these closely-knit and violent elements, sounding clear and tragic like brazen trumpets."[50]

Le Corbusier was therefore able both to understand Greek architecture and to avoid a most non-Greek imitation of it, precisely because he intuitively understood what it was meant to be and, further, because he recognized that it was not intended to shelter human beings, but to stir them to a recognition of the facts in relation to which they must act themselves. He himself loved action of all kinds, especially the modern gesture of movement. The long *autostrades* of his "Ville Contemporaine," of 1922 (plate 124), extended the Acropolis' central axis to the scale of the motor car, from which he was also able to derive inspiration, as from ships and airplanes.[53] His earliest buildings of the twenties created interiors that were stages for action. In his Ozenfant House, of 1922 (plate 125), the space is high and bare, made tumultuous and challenging by the projected library with its ship's ladder. The

41

furniture is light, cheap, and movable, meant to be used, and its active groupings in their high volume of space should be contrasted with Wright's architecturally scaled built-ins, in their low-scaled, interwoven environment (plate 40), and with Mies' frozen islands in space (plate 103a). In the light of these considerations, Le Corbusier's statement, so often misunderstood, "We must look upon a house as a machine for living in [machine à habiter] or as a tool . . . as serviceable as a typewriter [machine à écrire] . . ."[54] is seen to have been a purely man-centered, humanistic one. It meant that a house was for use by men, and a place of action, not of illusory refuge.

Le Corbusier's buildings of the twenties were tautly stretched containers for dramatized, rather skittish action. Therefore, though treated as isolated sculptural objects, they were not at first potentially active in the sculpturally figural sense (plate 15). Nor, particularly, were they muscular analogies for the human body and thus potential embodiments of the human act. Le Corbusier's movement toward such sculptural analogy can be traced step by step. He had first to work out the appropriate kind of space, then the appropriate structure, then finally to unify the two into a sculptural form to which they were both visually subordinated. It should be pointed out that the Doric temple had followed exactly this line of development; but Le Corbusier's problem was infinitely more complicated. For example, he hoped from the beginning to build large apartment houses, the essential housing type of a mass urban civilization. Each of the apartments in his first large project, of 1922, was like a separate villa, with a two-storied living room. Not expecting to see this project accepted or realized, he had already tried to work out each apartment as a free-standing house, which he called the "Citrohan Type." The background of these houses is obvious. They are essentially Mycenaean megara, pure space-containers, with three closed planes and one wall of glass. Le Corbusier then built a mock-up of the type for his Pavillon de l'Esprit Nouveau, of 1925. But as a free-standing object the megaron was inactive, being a simple box of space. In the Mycenaean palace it had been engulfed in a labyrinthine maze, and its descendant, the cella of the Greek temple, was screened, where possible, by a peripteral colonnade which made the building a free-standing sculptural force. For this reason Le Corbusier, as at Stuttgart in 1927, placed his megaron on legs, the *pilotis*, precisely to make it stand up (plate 126). Here the free-standing

42

column, rejected in the continuous phase from Piranesi through Wright and the International Style, first reappeared as an essential element of a building's exterior.[55] But the "space," not the "matter," was still the visual positive of the design. The skin was still stretched around the volume, in the manner of the International Style, and the columns were only poles. The building therefore had few analogies to the human body, being both obviously hollow and rather insectile. By 1930–32, Le Corbusier had gone a step further. In the Swiss Dormitory he joined two opposites. Some of its *pilotis* are plastic and muscular, but the box of rooms above them, broiling in the sun, is expressed as pure membrane around a space (plate 127). What is dramatized is the sculpturally active column lifting its opposite, a static volume, into the air. The building is not yet an integrated sculptural image.

Le Corbusier's experiments of the thirties apparently attempted three things: to create a building more totally active, to unify that action into monumental form, and to make the whole more structurally massive and solid. His project for the Palace of the Soviets, of 1931, is one of his most interesting in view of the first two aims. It breaks completely out of the containing skin, and its structure is dramatized as a tumultuous set of active forces (plate 128). Below the monumental scale of the upper structure of arch and bents, with their hung ceilings, moves a whole lower structure, a forest of columns at smaller scale. Le Corbusier then attempts to unify the scattered masses by conceiving of them as forming a body, with a head, shoulders, waist, and hips, so that in plan an under-image, like a piece of African sculpture, curiously emerges (plate 129). One wonders whether the influence of Surrealism, with its unexpectedly appearing images, clearly present in Le Corbusier's painting at this time, was not being reflected here. Certainly, the model of his Centrosoyus, of 1928–35, for Moscow, when seen from above, evokes the image of a rather surrealist goblin (plate 130). But it is in the character of architecture that it must normally remain abstract; its images must be integral, not representational. So Le Corbusier dropped the overt image, but the figural intention behind it was to remain. His search for plastic weight now grew stronger. In his little week-end house of 1935 he used concrete vaults set on thick concrete lintels, supported in some places by columns, elsewhere by substantial planes of masonry wall (plate 131). The vaulted space, lighted partly from above, and the plastic weight of the structure, alike broke away from the rectangular boxes of the International Style and bore fruit in Le Corbusier's brick-walled, concrete-linteled houses of the fifties, such as the Maisons Jaoul at Neuilly (plates 132, 133) and the Sarabhai Villa at Ahmedabad. The lintels, brutally scaled, are now so thick that the brick walls can be irregularly placed beneath them, even upon them over voids. The system is thus both structurally integral and, in Le Corbusier's own term, "dynamic." At the same time, the mass of the roughly surfaced solids exerts a real pressure on the spaces they create, so that action, though still encouraged, is now rather realistically tested, as in Kahn's and Stirling's work (certainly derived from this), by the harsh structural fact of the environment around it. Indeed, it is at this point, and in this kind of solid building in common materials, that Wright, Le Corbusier, Aalto, and Kahn, despite the fundamental differences between them, all approach each other and seem to offer the most promising way out of academicism for the younger men. The future, in a general and even a vernacular sense, would seem to lie just here, in an architecture reinvested with the tenaciously physical force of the Western architectural tradition.

In his Unité d'Habitation, at Marseilles, finished in 1952, all the elements of Le Corbusier's own unique search for an active monumentality were finally brought together (plate 134). The structure is of poured concrete, left rough, thus intrinsically textured and plastic itself. Each megaron-like apartment has its own balcony which acts as a *brise-soleil* (plate 134). Because of this, the box of rooms can no longer be read as a skin around a hollow, as in the Swiss Pavilion (plates 135, 127). The building seems to have only those voids which are integral to the system of its solids. Therefore it can be seen primarily in neither structural, spatial, nor abstractly massive terms—neither as a mountain, nor a cage, nor a box—but only as an articulated, unified, sculptural body.[56] Although the individual apartment units are expressed, still, all use-scale elements, such as doors and windows, which normally make us read buildings not as sculptural creatures but as hollow containers for human activity, are suppressed, so that the building, like a Greek temple with its peripteral colonnade, has only sculptural scale. It thus stands upon its muscular legs as an image of human uprightness and dignifies all its individual units within a single embodiment of the monumental human force which makes them possible. The high space of each apartment looks out toward the mountains and the sea, and it is

44

in relation to the mountains and the sea that the building as a whole should be seen. This is the larger, Hellenic environment that it creates. So perceived, it is a humanist building, as we empathetically associate ourselves with it, in the contrasting landscape, as a standing body analogous to our own. The definition through "empathy" again derives from Geoffrey Scott, cited in relation to the Guaranty Building. Scott wrote of humanist architecture in 1914: "The center of that architecture was the human body; its method to transcribe in stone the body's favorable states; and the moods of the spirit took visible shape along its borders, power and laughter, strength and terror and calm"[57] (plate 136). Scott then went on: "Ancient architecture excels in its perfect definition; Renaissance architecture in the width and courage of its choice."[58] In these terms Le Corbusier would seem to have passed beyond choice, beyond Renaissance humanism, to the essentials of a more nakedly Greek "definition," as his Unité arrives at the embodiment of an act. The space-dominated, environmental continuity of the materialistically confident late nineteenth and early twentieth centuries, in which the image of man normally disappeared from architecture, was thus cast aside in favor of a new, mid-twentieth-century image of the embattled human presence in the world.

That presence, however, can hardly be so fixed or bounded as the Greek image of it was. Thus, at Ronchamp, Le Corbusier takes a further step. He shows us the two opposites of enclosure and action, and causes the building to transform itself from one to the other before our eyes (plates 137, 138-41). Both the non-Hellenic and Hellenic methods, and their meanings, are consciously explored and extended. The hooded chapels are "hairpin," apsidal megara which recall in plan and elevation not only Le Corbusier's drawings of the cavernous shape of the Serapieion at Hadrian's Villa (beloved by Wright), but also various neolithic earth sanctuaries on Sardinia which are related in shape to the Serapieion.[59] Around these the whole rear of the building turns (plate 138), bulging with its enclosed volumes as a pure container, but as it approaches the east that wall pushes back in upon the interior space and the pulpit swings outward like the clapper of a bell (plate 139). The roof slab is meanwhile both pressing down upon the interior and rising upward toward its southeast corner, toward which the south wall is also pushing in, curving out and rising (plate 140). Thus, from this side, the building is the opposite of the rear (plate 139). It cannot be read as a hollow shell around interior space (contrast the Guggenheim Museum) (plate 90), but only as a gathering force, which actively thrusts in and upward, and then, unlike the Greek temple, splits out of the Euclidean envelope in a lunge to the corner. Behind this the megaron of the highest chapel is seen, and at the southern, entrance side, the two opposites of container and actor are contrasted (plate 141). Between them is the door, threatened, because the building is divided above it and the slab has its farthest unsupported projection there. To the right the fortress-like wall, not structural at all, lifts upward toward its pointed apex. Again, its scattered windows must be as they are to allow it to act as a sculptural force. If they were too large, or lined up in horizontal rows, indicating floor levels, or in vertical panels, indicating that the wall was a screen, its purely sculptural unity and scale—and thus its power to act—would be lost. There is also a kind of irony in this anthropological demonstration and this juxtaposition of opposites, as there is in the fortress which is no fortress and in the challenging door. Although the church, in its union of cavern with thrusting force, is an appropriate embodiment of the Virgin to whom it is dedicated ("Spiritual Vessel . . . Tower of David . . . House of Gold . . . Tower of Ivory," the Litany calls her), it is most of all an image of modern man, full of memories, with an ironic view of himself, no longer believing that he occupies the center of the world by right. He is under pressure in the interior of Ronchamp (plate 140), which does not swell outward from him but presses in upon him. As in Le Corbusier's Modulor (plate 142)—in contrast to the static Vitruvian system which contains him perfectly so long as he does not stir—he can only act, or gesture; and that act, like the Fibonacci series of the Modulor, or the upward lifting prow of Ronchamp on its hilltop, has no defined boundary and is open-ended toward the ultimate reaches of space.

46

On the other hand, that act must be understood in relation to nature's law, which is separate from it, possibly hostile to it, but which, for us as for the Greeks, is real. This is what Le Corbusier seems to show most poignantly in his Monastery of La Tourette, which seeks to keep its footing on the slope, encloses its tight court full of geometric symbols, and lifts its monks' cells to the far horizon (plate 143). In this way the natural landscape takes on a dimension and dignity far greater than it had possessed when its forms, as in Wright's work, lost their separate being and were drawn into the shifting human condition by being echoed and abstracted in the "pathetic fallacy" of human emotion. Now the landscape is left alone to be itself, the constant measure of the acts of men, who change and suffer upon it. Le Corbusier had apparently hoped to explore these relationships in his rejected scheme for St. Dié, and he is now realizing them at Chandigarh. There his general plan for the city, unlike the romantic-naturalist Garden City type of Mayer and Whittlesey's first project, is a kind of combination of romantic-classic and romantic-naturalist modes. Regular squares define the neighborhoods, but irregularly shaped green areas flow through them. Order and freedom are in this sense combined, and a more "classic" wholeness, not a "classicizing" restriction, is attained.[60] At the north is the vast plaza which is formed by the buildings of the capitol complex itself, seen against the backdrop of the Himalayas to the north (plate 144). Here a related combination occurs: between "space-positive" and "solid-positive" group design. The Secretariat and the High Court are space-definers, like Greek stoas, but, unlike the stoa, they are active forces as well, while, as in a Greek agora, the more purely mid-space buildings are placed in the void they define. On the city side, long mounds of earth make the capitol look as if it were actually within the mountains, but upon a closer approach these fall behind and the true scale of the relationship is grasped. To the left the elongated block of the Secretariat bounds the space and leads the eye toward the northern ridge lines, while the long slant of the form on its roof increases the velocity of that movement (plate 145). Below it the regular grid of offices is interrupted by the curving mass of a ramp housing. This is pulled out as if to show the building's insides, while beyond it the major offices break away from the regular grid system, confuse the structural definitions, and thus plastically reveal, with a dilation like breath, the controlling center of the building's active life. Mid-space, seen against the mountains as an isolated form, the final version of the Assembly Hall is made to gesture toward the center of the plaza (the first version was statically symmetrical), while the otherwise concealed volume of its meeting room thrusts up through the roof to call to the mountains' hollows and ridges beyond it (plate 146). The original design for the Governor's Palace, most actively profiled element of all, and meant to be placed directly ahead against the mountains, may not be built, but the High Court still bounds the plaza on the east side (plate 144). It is thrust northward of the Assembly Building, so that it again enforces the view toward the mountains, and the horizontal roof line of the strict envelope in which it is contained carries the eye toward them, indicating once more the real boundaries of the space (plates 2, 123). Within this frame the High Court is a great, hollowed-out, concrete mass (plate 147). Its glass skin is again masked, on the entrance side, by a *brise-soleil* which keeps the scale integral and pushes upward and out with threatening power (plate 148). Up through this projection, continued further upward by the hung vaults of the canopy, rise the great piers as purely upward-thrusting forces. Between these, men enter, and ramps of an almost Piranesian violence rise behind them (plate 149). Their physical power can be grasped if we compare them with Paul Rudolph's entrance for his second High School, in Sarasota, Florida (plate 150), which was, as the architect freely admits, inspired by them. The American design has become thin, planar, and linear. It is tautly stretched as a parasol against the sun, and cannot be read as analogous to the confident human body, assuming position in a place, as Le Corbusier's demands to be.[59] Moreover, if we compare the High Court's piers with the columns of the House of German Art in Munich (plates 151, 152), we can best understand why Le Corbusier has been able to create a convincingly monumental architecture in modern terms and why the Nazis and, indeed, many other power groups, were not able to do so with their columned façades. The latter are inert, not monumental, because they do not value the individual act; but Le Corbusier's aggrandize the man who stands before them by stretching his own force empathetically upward with them (plate 145). In this way, in balance with the landscape forms, they embody the human act of authority in the Court.

Men thus return to the earth as men. They no longer either ignore it for a dream of ideal formal or mechanical perfection or seek to evade human identification by dissolving into it through the other, "natural," or evolutionary, dreams. They appear to reject perfect protection and mobility alike—so leave the cave, come off the road, forsake the river, and take a stand. This seems the fullest realization in architecture so far of the new humanity, self-governing and expecting no favors, which first began to be imagined two hundred years ago and sought its ancestry in Greece: "a shaft . . . inflexible and free."

3   TWELVE YEARS AFTER:
The Age of Irony

"The wrecks beside of many a city vast,
Whose population which the earth grew over
Was mortal, but not human; see, they lie,
Their monstrous works,…"
— PERCY BYSSHE SHELLEY, *Prometheus Unbound*

"As April's green endures; or will endure"
WALLACE STEVENS, *Sunday Morning*

This addition to the text offers an opportunity not only to focus on the major new developments in architecture since 1960 but also, in the light of those events, to revise and enlarge the view of modern architectural history as a whole which the original text presented. This typical historical process of interaction between past and present has been especially complex and important during these years. A sad but highly instructive decade has intervened between the previous page and this one. The heroic note upon which the former ended was not a spurious one, but it carried the hybris of its own destruction with it. Like Kennedy's first, and only, Inaugural Address, it culminated a period of social and political drift which had, however, also nurtured an existential idealism in individual thought, and it aimed to translate that kind of philosophy into heroic action during the decade to come—the one just past. In the political sphere, the premises upon which such action was eventually based turned out, unfortunately, to be mistakenly confrontational and empirically out of date. This is not the place to trace the sequence of crimes and follies which ultimately ensued and through which, under the guidance of progressively less balanced men, the most influential nation of the modern world was brought to the edge of moral, and hence social and political, disaster. At the same time the vitality of its arts was by no means impaired, in an expressive if not necessarily a programmatic sense, and they not only tell the decade's story with enormous clarity but also offer several suggestions for more reasonable action in the future.

49

They must therefore occupy much of the center of the stage, though I hope not all of it, in any consideration of the 1960s on an international level.

The tragic drama may properly be said to have gotten underway in architecture with Paul Rudolph's Art and Architecture Building for Yale University.[62] Rudolph's mood at that moment was one of heroic confrontation; he was at last ready to take the European masters on (plate 153). Hence he exaggerated the lift of the High Court at Chandigarh and of La tourette (plates 143, 151), and he ingeniously squeezed and distorted various functions to do so. His building is beautifully sited, but it is also disturbingly aggressive; its hammer-bashed, striated concrete is visually expressive but physically dangerous, more truly "sadomasochistic" than its High Victorian progenitors[63] (Fig. 20). Over the decade since its completion most of its students have rightly or wrongly come to regard it as the prime symbol of an unnecessarily competitive attitude toward people and things. It clearly demonstrated, at least, some of the programmatic limitations of the sculpturally-active mode of building. Probably only Le Corbusier himself was able to accomplish that kind of figural embodiment without doing considerable violence to spatial and functional requirements.

By 1965, at any rate, it was obvious that the confrontational stance had entered a bureaucratized and brutalized phase. The methods and products of American Redevelopment were its offspring, as was the war in Vietnam. A government center proposed in 1966 for New Haven (plate 154), just down the street and across the Green from Rudolph's Art School, would have frozen the forms no less than the concept of Le Corbusier's High Court into an empty and unfeeling image of sterile power, so creating another of those "empty landscapes of psychosis" about which Norman Mailer warned us in 1963.[64] Everything— including, say, Lincoln Center of the same years—was in fact beginning to look more like the Deutsches Museum (plate 152) than the High Court. Indeed, the most purely governmental monuments of "modern architecture" in the States in more recent days have all become unmistakably totalitarian in character. The Johnson Library in Austin, Texas, and the projected Hirschorn Museum in Washington, are chilling examples. Again, their architectural model was an old one, and hazardously out of date.

The same was true of the model in planning when Redevelopment got under way in the late fifties. That model was fundamentally Le Corbusier's Ville Radieuse. In New Haven, the link with Le Corbusier was a direct one, in the person of Maurice Rotival, who decided that the "Thruways" should be brought right through the city, exactly as Le Corbusier had proposed a generation before (plates 124, 155). Suburbanites and central-city businessmen were to profit. The fabric of the center of the city, with its buildings of many ages, its streets, sidewalks, and multiplicity of functions, was to be cataclysmically blasted out in favor of a puristically conceived new world of connectors, superblocks, and free-standing towers. The automobile triumphed, and the heart of the city became a suburban shopping center too.[65] The urban poor who had inhabited the area were not part of the governmentally subsidized system (which might accurately be described as middle-class socialism) and were moved out to make way for it. Some, mostly black, were removed several times—to react at last in the urban disorders of the late sixties; in New Haven in 1967.

The architectural and planning model, though seductive to the old American loves for mobility and abstract order alike (plates 23, 24, 155), had demonstrably failed to conform to enough of the human facts of present urban reality. How to start again? Here the work of Louis Kahn occupies a very special position during the decade. On the one hand its monumental geometry, whatever its background in Kahn's early Beaux-Arts training, was part of the heroic idealism of the fifties.[66] Its planning proposals, for example, were no less cataclysmic than those of Le Corbusier, if rather more fanciful (plate 156). On the other hand, Kahn had also begun to rethink the problems of building in a systematic way and to move ponderously beyond preconceived models. For a time he thus broke out into a new empiricism and was able to create strong new forms through a fresh analysis of function and structure. He was at first most successful in the latter category, as his Medical Laboratories showed (plates 120–122). There the functions, though elaborately analyzed, turned out in practice to be impoverished by tight spaces, lack of sun protection, and so on, despite which the precast concrete structure continues to move the viewer with the systematic order and dignity of its assemblage. But in Kahn's Unitarian Church for Rochester (plates 157, 158), all the hard and solemn shapes were now derived from an analysis of function and, most of all, from the reception of light: two stories of glare-protected windows

51

for classrooms and so on around the periphery, four great monitors to flood a splendid radiance across the Brutalist concrete skeleton and the cinder-block walls of the central meeting room.[67] Here, and in other buildings such as his dormitories at Bryn Mawr and the Jonas B. Salk Center for Biological Research in California, Kahn may be said to have gone far toward liberating architecture from its contemporary preconceptions and, in his own solid brick and concrete constructions, to have shaped some of the major monuments of the modern age. And his buildings are monuments in a very traditional sense. They are more rigidly and intricately geometric in space and massing than the general run of that New Brutalist production which Kahn's design had played its part in forming (plates 122, 132). Released from glazing, for which Kahn had little feeling (preferring pure voids in solids), and indeed from modern technology as a whole, they entered a kind of expansively baroque phase in the capitol for East Pakistan at Dacca and the Indian Institute of Management at Ahmedabad (plate 159). They, too, recall both their direct Roman models in Trajan's Market and Ostia Antica, and Piranesi and his pervasive modern resurrections as well (plates 3–8). That formalistic euphoria also recalls Le Corbusier's on the subcontinent (plate 148). Le Corbusier's buildings had been modeled for sculptural plasticity (plate 151), but it was a no less massive drama of structural articulation that Kahn developed. And so his later buildings have normally remained: eloquent expressions of space and structure which invoke traditional stabilities and are unconcerned with any symbolism of the immediate present or with the technology or the ambiguities of contemporary life.

In a sense, Kahn became the new hero-architect of the early sixties, perhaps the last such creator-formgiver that we shall see. With the passing of the heroes, the Age of Romanticism passes, Romantic-Classicism and Romantic-Naturalism alike. The new age (let us say the new moment) can hardly yet be named, but all the arts of its early years suggest that the Age of Irony so far describes it.[68] Kahn, like Le Corbusier, indeed did something to bring it about—Kahn especially in his role as the most productive teacher of the late fifties and early sixties. It was one of his many students and collaborators, Robert Venturi, who took a first step into the new age, and toward the revitalization of architectural conceptions, programs, and forms. It was a giant step, because it finally disavowed idealism and architectural heroics alike in favor of a renewed, if rather ironic, acceptance of reality and a new realistic symbolism, and it moved toward what can only be called a "semeiological" intention in design.[69] Here the building "wants" (to use one of Kahn's expressions) not so much to express structure and space as to signify what it means in terms of its social use and urbanistic function. So Venturi's Guild House (plate 160), where the frontispiece employs arched wall-forms of a type first used by Kahn, now exploits that flat surface to define the street and to lift continuously upward to the symbolic television aerial (it is not the functioning aerial) which at once culminates that movement like a classical akroterion and also describes with considerable accuracy what generally goes on inside. Giving back diagonally behind this signpost, the windows offer various descriptions of the functions of the rooms themselves and then bring the back plane forward by increasing their scale. The whole thus deals with the facts of modern life at a level not only functional but physically active and symbolic. It respects the traditional street no less than the common techniques of building. In these ways it breaks with the doctrinaire purism of the modern movement in planning as well, and the "idealistically" cataclysmic super-block methods of Redevelopment are as explicitly contradicted by it as are the titanic structural agonies of the New Brutalism itself (plates 132, 136). "Main Street is almost all right," Venturi wrote in his important book, *Complexity and Contradiction in Architecture*, of 1966.[70] As he did so, the past no less than the present changed. This is always the case in history. A new concept opens our eyes to aspects of past experience that had temporarily dropped out of focus. So in the first edition of this book I concentrated, for example, on Louis Sullivan's skyscrapers (plates 30, 32), surely in part because they were prototypical of Le Corbusier and Mies (plates 100, 101, 134, 135), and left out (only in part through the limitations of space) any reference to his village banks in brick, which had grown directly out of the vernacular forms of Main Street and had ennobled without changing them[71] (plate 161). So the base, in Venturi's building as in Sullivan's, lifts the façade above the automobiles, while the old American false front or its equivalent rises to give a monumental shape to the space of the street as a whole.

Following this renewed perception for traditional street architecture and for semeiological imagery, other aspects of the past now came into view.[72] Michel de Klerk's great works of the

Amsterdam school, in part Expressionist after Gaudi (plates 47–50), in part English Queen Anne, but mostly pure Dutch, must now be included here: they were, alas, left out before.[73] The long, squat Post Office of De Klerk's Public Utility Housing of 1918 is a chugging, piston-pushing, wheel-spinning locomotive (plate 162), pulling its stretched, horizontally-segmented block of buildings down the street behind it like a string of cars. It is in fact set along the railroad track, and drops manfully behind or flashes mightily past as the real trains go by.

Again, semeiologically, our eyes are opened to the splendid low cost public housing which was built more or less along lines like those explored by De Klerk by the social democratic city government of Vienna during the nineteen twenties. Its heroes were the great Mayors, Jakob Reumann and Karl Seitz, and a whole host of dedicated public officials, some of whom were martyred in and after the Rightist *Putsch* of 1934. Their noble memorials, the *Gemeindebauten*, were constructed of stuccoed bearing walls and were planned both to define the city's streets and to create ever more generous block-sized courtyards, providing gardens, child-care centers, dental clinics, laundries, schools, and swimming pools. More than 62,000 units were built before 1934, when almost everything stopped; but by that time they had helped reduce deaths by tuberculosis from 33 in 10,000 in 1913 to 16 (in 1930), and infant mortality from 15.5 percent to 7.22 percent, and rents from 30 to 6 or 8 percent of a workman's salary.[74] The contrast with the aims and methods of American Redevelopment could hardly be more striking. The most eloquent masterpiece among the groups was surely Karl Ehn's Heiligenstadt Houses (the Karl Marx Hof) of 1927–1930—a mighty fortress, where the major facade is a proud, dark banner of socialist solidarity (plate 163). It was to be stormed alike by the troops of Dollfuss and the Red Army. It clearly infuriated many people, a little bit as the Guild House does today, but its powerful shapes, Piranesian on the exterior but much more gently articulated in the lovely garden courtyards, in fact historically culminate and bring to an enormous social climax the special Viennese tradition of Otto Wagner and his school.[75] The scale is grander, like that of all the Viennese housing, than that of the Guild House (plate 160), but the two buildings are related insofar as they both gesture like signboards to tell us what they are about. How correct the gentle irony of the American example is in this particular instance, and how stirring the Austrian's triumphant deployment: in simple political fact daring hell and surviving. Yet its forms could hardly have been adapted to the America of the 1960s. The way of life had changed beyond European recognition; the Karl Marx Hof was pre-worker-automobile most of all. It thus inhabited the pre-Le Corbusier urban environment of Camillo Sitte. Venturi takes the same elements, supergraphics, flags, and frontispieces, and shows us the actual scale of most contemporary American life and symbolism: that of the superhighway, the Strip, and the suburb (plate 164). Here Pop Art, totally unknown, at least to me, when I wrote the first edition of this book, has played its part in blowing up the scale of everyday vernacular forms and so projecting them as monuments. The ultimate Californian image, the magic "Hollywood" print of Edward Ruscha, is prefigured by Venturi here. Probably only an American can understand how things like these can stir the heart: the high desert, the days of driving, the big cars—though it took a Russian exile, Nabokov, writing in *Lolita*, and after him the Texan, Larry McMurtry, to endow them with their present dreamlike, ironically mythic aura.

So the United States, in the persons of some of its writers, painters, sculptors, architects, and movie-makers, began by the middle sixties to find an experiential way out of the paranoid exploitation of its myths toward an emotional grasp of their realities: the first necessary step toward improving them, if it seemed desirable to do so. The shameful failure in public housing had to be recognized. In contrast, the Viennese accomplishment, coming from a bankrupt republic after a massive military defeat and the total loss of an empire, was almost too much to contemplate. It is painful, for example, to watch American architects like Charles Moore attempting (for, it must be said, an urban poor tied to the city by poverty and discrimination rather than by solidarity or desire) to achieve some shadow of the common spatial amenities, community services, and urban scale which the Viennese budget allowed[76] (plates 165, 166). Considering what he had to work with, Moore has done marvelously well indeed. Again, in forms like these from the twenties, largely outside the International Style and hence previously underestimated by us, we can now see prototypes for some of the work of the younger American architects, as for that of Alvar Aalto who was, along with Kahn, the most influential of their immediate masters, and whose own work continues surpassingly rich, varied, and humane (plates 113–118).

55

The civilized command of public housing emphatically remained a European rather than an American achievement in the sixties and early seventies. An architect like Emile Aillaud had not only learned the Dutch and Austrian lessons well but also had available to him the public funds which were necessary to carry them out (plate 167). The precast mosaic wall panels of his most recent projects around Paris not only solve problems of budget and mass production but also create a taut, closed, brightly glowing surface which is a kind of technological rationalization of the rich Dutch and Austrian brick, masonry, and stucco examples.[77] His varied site planning, too, seems to owe something to Austria, while the sculptural and pictorial imagery with which he humanizes his squares is related to the Pop Art of Oldenburg and others no less than the work of Venturi is.

England, too, has produced magnificent public housing. Roehampton (plate 168) should have been illustrated in the earlier edition of this book.[78] Built by the London County Council, and employing many fine younger architects who were soon to become distinguished on their own, it is surely the most successful Corbusian housing group in the world—probably because its apartment slabs and its (rather more Scandinavian) tower blocks are set exactly as Le Corbusier would have liked to have sited all his housing (plate 127): in an actual *jardin anglais*, in this case Richmond Park on the outskirts of London. Yet again, in the sixties, that Corbusian pattern was challenged in ways that recalled older experiences hitherto forgotten. In this case it was Russian Constructivism which came alive once more, just as the Soviet Union itself began to stir with life for a while after Stalin's death in 1953. The House of Industry in Kharkov, of 1925–35, is an example of the excitement about urban life and technology with which Russian Constructivism was endowed[79] (plate 169). Bridges connect towers high in space; the multilevel city, Metropolis, masses densely upward and throws roadways across the void; it is all very different from the isolated towers standing in the gardens of the Ville Radieuse. I left Russian Constructivism out of the first edition, even though Le Corbusier's project for the Palace of the Soviets of 1931 (plate 128), strongly evoked that movement just at the moment when the Stalinist reaction was out to destroy it on ideological grounds. I left it out, I suppose, because the International Style, though it owed much to Russian Constructivism, had in fact abandoned most of its character, especially its crude daring and its positive, violent joy in the human density and the technological challenges of modern life. The Bauhaus, despite somewhat similar intentions in the beginning (plates 68–70), eventually bowdlerized all that revolutionary excitement into good, small-scaled, German bourgeois "design." But the background of Constructivism lay in the fevered north Italian, Futurist visions of Marinetti and Sant' Elia and beyond them in the romantically competitive Beaux-Arts skyscrapers of New York, of which, still involved with Sullivan and Le Corbusier, I said not enough in the first edition. Cass Gilbert's Woolworth Building (1913) is probably the finest of them all.[80] But it is as they group together that the skyscrapers have most captured the imagination of the world, rising upward as they do in massed spires, connected in architects' visions at least by roads in the sky, and crowned with airships out of H. G. Wells (plates 81, 170). So the mighty housing group at Sheffield, of the 1960s (plate 171), used an elevated corridor-roadway, of a type suggested by Peter and Alison Smithson, to link its long slabs together through the air.[81] The corridor takes wing, but as the hill slopes upward it often returns close to grade and so provides a marvelous freedom of movement into and through the buildings.

Russian Constructivism had yet another fundamental characteristic, which the new work of the sixties has also rediscovered and helped us see. It too was supremely "semeiological" in the simplest sense: meant to tell a story, to spread words as well as images across the sky, to become what has been called "an informational appliance."[82] So the airships of King's Dream of New York are hitched by Vesnin's diagonal cables to carry banners of "Battle and Victory" in 1919 (plate 172). In their shadow whole cities are strung together by wires. Old solid masses topple except as the new tense strings hold them up. This was the revolutionary Constructivist vision, of ancient weights overthrown and everything suspended, dancing in the wind, held on a web of wire (plate 173). It could hardly have been built, at least not in Russia in 1919, but the image was there and that was the great thing. We see it again in Oldenburg today (plate 174). The old city of London is suddenly changed when a technological and here also a stunningly common form (a toilet float) is blown up tremendously in scale, gilded, and floated like a sun on the Thames, to rise and fall with the tide.[83]

It does not seem likely that such projects will normally find fulfillment soon, but some of the best buildings of the sixties

57

were also freshly imbued with their spirit. Stirling and Gowan's Engineering Laboratory for Leicester University (plate 175) was a distinguished example early in the decade.[84] Its sense of suspension and its excitement over industrial materials and processes were united with a kind of space which was primarily that of tubes or laboratories, as of a man-circulating machine rather than a traditionally volumetric building. Its major special spaces in the cantilevered lecture rooms seem specifically to refer, perhaps through the mediation of a Dutch example,[85] to an actual Russian building of the twenties: Melnikov's famous Workers' Clubhouse with its projecting classrooms and bold signs (plate 176). Stirling and Gowan's building is even more visually Constructivist than the Russian prototype, probably in part because the technology to make physical realities out of some of the earlier visions had actually come into being by this time. But that technology was instantly pressed to new visionary dimensions by the young English architects of the sixties. The Living City Exposition in London, of 1963 (plate 177), was surely one of the significant image-makers of recent times.[86] Here Peter Cook and his followers, who came to call their largely graphic work Archigrams, imagined science-fiction systems of plug-in environments in which various kinds of space pods were to be slid in and out of demountable frames and hooked up to utilities and life-support devices of every conceivable kind. Unlike their distinguished Soviet progenitors, who may be said to have combined the old romanticism of the machine with a kind of romantic revolutionism, the new generation presents its ideas with considerable aerospace playacting and a kind of neo-Futurist pseudo-fury, and so modernizes the older attitude with the contemporary ironic sense. The influence of their designs has already produced international competition winners which are now in the agonized throes of redesign for purposes of construction. The Plateau Beaubourg Project in Paris, by Rogers, Piano, *et al.*, is an outstanding example.

58

The vitality in the Archigrammist concepts is related to that in Venturi's work, despite the tremendous difference in the resultant forms and in spite of the rather shrill ridicule with which some of the technologically-obsessed English critics have greeted his considerably subtler, if often annoyingly phrased, ideas. In both cases it has to do with the symbolic and again somewhat ironic acceptance of modern life, so that what was once distasteful or threatening to us is caught and humanized through art: by which we are liberated from ignorance and fear to act anew. With Venturi it is the vulgar environment of Strip and Main Street; with the English it is technology's rogue force and the crowded future that looms over us all. A bit of that vision has helped knock some major American work out of its otherwise rigidly poweristic doldrums, so that Roche and Dinkeloo's Coliseum (plate 178), in contrast to their Knights of Columbus Building alongside, takes on a strong measure of Constructivism's or Archigram's skeletal daring and science-fiction scale, though only a touch of their dynamism and hectic wit.

The Japanese, embedded as they are at this very moment in a mortally packed and polluted urban environment, have understood the challenge perfectly well. Their visionary group, close to the Archigrammists, calls itself Metabolist and moves in much the same neo-Constructivist direction, which seems now to be followed in general by the best known architects in Japan.[87] Kenzo Tange, for example, housing his Yamanashi Communications Center (plate 179) in what is simply a traditional single building of Brutalist concrete, brings it to life by trying to make it look like a developing Archigrammist system, with spatial units slung between supporting towers which purport to be in various stages of structural process in plan and elevation alike. It is probably here that Roche and Dinkeloo went wrong when they classicized the similar towers of their Knights of Columbus Building into a fixed, symmetrical form.[88] Their scale is too big for that; to be effective they must suggest the Metabolist promise of a whole new enormous environment growing.

In his undoubtedly over-praised Habitat (plate 180), Moshe Safdie attempted similar effects, but there the heavy reinforced concrete structure was surely fighting the general conception, where the apartment volumes really "wanted" to be light, demountable, and fixed in a frame.[89] Paul Rudolph would have accomplished this synthesis of intention and method in his Graphic Arts Center project for Manhattan, of 1969, where his grandiose challenge to the existing environment was technologically rationalized in peculiarly American terms by the projected use of actual mobile homes (Magnolia Mobile Homes from Vicksburg, Mississippi) which were to have been wheeled up from their southern factory, slung in a structural armature, and plugged into the mechanical systems.[90] It was pure Archigram, but buildable. Like Safdie's grouping, however, it moved toward the setback, more or less pyramidal massing of the pueblos of the

59

American Southwest rather than either the vertical Hellenic bodies represented by the towers of Sullivan, Mies, and Le Corbusier (plates 32, 100, 134), or the machine-like leaps of Archigrammist composition. The Great Houses of the Pueblos are themselves a massing of single-room units, stepped back to allow a terrace for each level and eventually also, I think, to echo the shapes of their sacred mountains rather than, like Greek temples, to contrast with them.[91] The difference between those two conceptions of the human position in the world is probably the fundamental distinction between the two editions of the present work, and indeed between the old and new ages, those of the fifties and the seventies, as a whole. Events have forced us toward a humbler and perhaps more analytical view of ourselves and a gentler stance in relation to other human beings and to the outside world.[92]

Baffled by such cosmic considerations, we can at least focus some attention on the Mobile Home. One out of every four dwellings produced each year in the United States is a mobile home. (It was one out of five when I wrote *American Architecture and Urbanism* in 1969). Cheaply and often shoddily built, they are still perfectly equipped for modern living—the life-support pod complete—and in economic terms they offer the only bargain on the American housing market today. This has to be the case because they are so integral a development out of everything we most believe in and can handle well: mass production, mobility, the automobile. Even when it costs a dollar a mile to move them with a trailer tractor, what might be called the imminence of movement is still there. In reality, the worker is not so tied to a place in a mobile home as he is in the traditional house. His equity is less; his market, as for a used car, wider; and in the present unsettled state of economics and automation he may well need to be able to sell and move on. Through the mobile home modern technology in the form of the automobile assembly line begins to sneak up (and high time, too) upon the American home-building industry, slipping past realtors, unions, zoning boards, fine arts commissions, past everything in fact which is interested in preserving the environmental status quo. It is a typically American revolution, but, curiously enough, the canonical size of the mobile home in breadth and usually in height is just about that of the apartment unit for the Unité d'Habitation which Le Corbusier worked out a generation ago and slung in its heroic frame (plates 134–136).

All such frames may be obsolescent now, just as the framework of the lives we have known is crumbling around us. So mobile homes should be seen in their own groupings, separate but placed quite close together and hence economical in land use and, so interviews and direct experience show, highly successful in creating a healthier sense of community than most suburbs seem to possess.[93] Yet I cannot resist illustrating a night wagon ring (plate 181) not of average mobile homes but of the great Airstream trailers, beautifully built of aluminum with tautly curved details that should delight Jean Prouvé,[94] but smaller (up to 31 feet) than most mobile homes and capable of sustained mobility behind an automobile.

Perhaps much architecture of the future will be really movable, packaged, combat-loaded for fast erection, and inflated to a silver cloud like the glowing project for a mobile theater (plate 182) produced by De Bretteville, Hodgetts, et al.[95] On the other hand, if we have learned anything during the last decade it is that we need reject nothing and should avoid puristic solutions to anything. Charles Moore has called the newly evolving architecture of the sixties "inclusive" rather than "exclusive" like the old International Style model.[96] The individual architectural monument is also apparently most effective at present in small-scale, ironic terms. So Venturi: he learns from the Strip and its signs[97] and, where such is appropriate, builds a fire station that gestures like a sign to tell us that this is the home of mighty Number 4 (plate 183), ready to rush out and do battle, but sympathetic and common too, as everybody knows. The openings of different sizes express the different functions; across and ignoring them the white brick pulls the whole mass into its single, actively gesturing, semeiological unity of communication on the highway.

Or on Nantucket, floated on a dream, where the cool fogs off the North Atlantic drift silently around the old grey houses, Venturi creates a totally different and equally valid image of America, of the empty horizon, the lonely island, and the Viking sea (plate 184). In doing so he makes direct use not only of the placement of the Greek temples at Selinunte, but also of the American tradition of wooden houses and especially and most consciously of the Shingle Style (plate 35).[98] But now the houses stand up, very tense, taut, and lonely, like individuals trying to speak to each other, Americans in their predicament here. Can this be that progress which the modern age has hitherto insisted upon? Is there progress in art? Or in the inner life of human beings? Scott Fitzgerald—foolish, snobbish and, with Bogart, the culture hero of the decade in question—somehow knew all about it: "So we beat on," he wrote in *Gatsby*, "boats against the current, borne back ceaselessly into the past."

It would be irresponsible to end without another word in regard to those major suggestions for a viable future which the decade just gone by seems to have offered. Commonsense realism and technological imagination, yes, with plenty of irony to sweeten our pretensions, and a lively vernacular in all of those many artifacts from buildings to automobiles, streets, parks, and rapid transit lines, which create the human environment entire. Such must surely be architecture's major attitude and concern from now on. But that comfortable urbanistic truism finally compels us to face the single fundamental question, which has to do with program and clientele. Who is it for? Who owns it? In answer, it is obvious that the needs of everyone will have to be served much better in the future, and upon a broader base of decision and ownership than that, for example, upon which Redevelopment in America foundered. It seems clear that effective public sovereignty, with some form of community responsibility and control, more humanely democratic than the totalitarian systems or than the middle-class socialism of the sixties, will be as necessary for the future of architecture as for all other aspects of mass human life.[99] The history of the past decade (with perhaps the brave image of Vienna behind that) indicates that the salvation of the earth's environment, and the possibility for sane human action within it, will both hinge upon that civilizing development. Whether the world will in fact move toward it rather than toward bureaucratic repression remains the large open question. The United States under its present administration, with its political write-off of the urban poor, is most ominously not doing so.

1.   Specchi and De Sanctis. Spanish Stairs, Rome, 1721–25.

2.   Le Corbusier. High Court, Chandigarh, India, 1951–56. Perspective drawing in landscape.

3. Giovanni Battista Piranesi. Plate 15 from the Carceri series, 2nd state, 1744–45 and 1760–61.

4. Sir John Soane. Bank of England, Old Dividend Office, London, 1818–23.

5. *John Paxton. Crystal Palace, the Telescope Gallery, London, 1851.*

6. *Ferdinand Dutert. International Exposition, Galerie des Machines, Paris, 1889.*

7.   Max Berg. Centennial Hall, Breslau, 1913.

8.   Nowicki and Dietrick. Livestock Pavilion, Raleigh, North Carolina, 1953.

9. *Pier Luigi Nervi and A. Vitellozzi. Palazzetto dello Sport, Rome, 1957.*

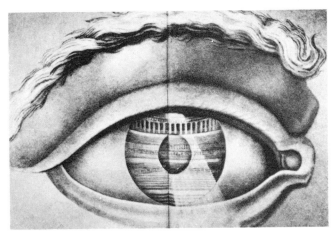

10. *Claude-Nicolas Ledoux. Théatre de Besançon. Symbolic representation of the Salle de Spectacles, 1778–84.*

12. *Tower of the Winds, Athens. Drawing by Stuart and Revett, 1762.*

11. *Ludwig and Franz Ruff. Reichs Congress Hall, Nuremberg, 1936.*

13.   Claude-Nicolas Ledoux. House designs, after 1773.

14.   Thomas Jefferson. University of Virginia, Charlottesville, Virginia, 1819–26. Engraving of 1856.

15.   Le Corbusier. Villa Savoie, Poissy-sur-Seine, 1929–30.

16. *Mique and H. Robert. Le Hameau, Versailles, 1782.*

17. *Dudley Newton. Sturtevant House, Middletown, Rhode Island, 1872.*

18. *Harwell Hamilton Harris. Johnson House, Los Angeles, California, 1949.*

19. Leo von Klenze. Valhalla, Regensburg, 1830–42.

20. William Butterfield. All Saints Church,
Margaret Street, London, 1849–59.

21. Visconti and Lefuel. Pavillon Colbert,
Louvre, Paris, 1852–57.

22. Charles Garnier. L'Opéra, Paris, 1861–74.

23. "Across the Continent," 1868. Colored lithograph by F. Peters after J. M. Ives.

24. John Augustus Roebling. Brooklyn Bridge, New York, 1867–83. Contemporary print.

25.   Henry Hobson Richardson. Watts-Sherman House, Newport, Rhode Island, 1874–76.

26.   Henry Hobson Richardson. Stoughton House, Cambridge, Massachusetts, 1882–83

27. *Henry Hobson Richardson. Ames Gate Lodge, North Easton, Massachusetts, 1880–81.*

28. *Henry Hobson Richardson. Marshall Field Warehouse, Chicago, Illinois, 1885–87.*

29. Adler and Sullivan. Walker Warehouse,
Chicago, Illinois, 1888–89.

30. Adler and Sullivan. Wainwright Building,
St. Louis, Missouri, 1890–91.

31. D. H. Burnham and J. W. Root. Reliance
Building, Chicago, Illinois, 1890–94.

32.   *Adler and Sullivan. Guaranty Building, Buffalo, New York, 1895.*

33.   *Louis Sullivan. Carson, Pirie and Scott Department Store, Chicago, Illinois, 1899–1904.*

34. Wilson Eyre. Ashurst House, Overbrook, Pennsylvania, ca. 1885.

35. Bruce Price. Kent House, Tuxedo Park, New York, 1885–86.

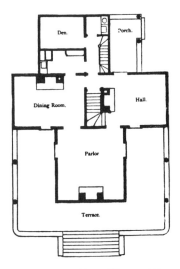

35a. Kent House. Plan.

36. *Frank Lloyd Wright. Ward Willitts House, Highland Park, Illinois, 1900–02.*

37. *Ward Willitts House. Plan.*

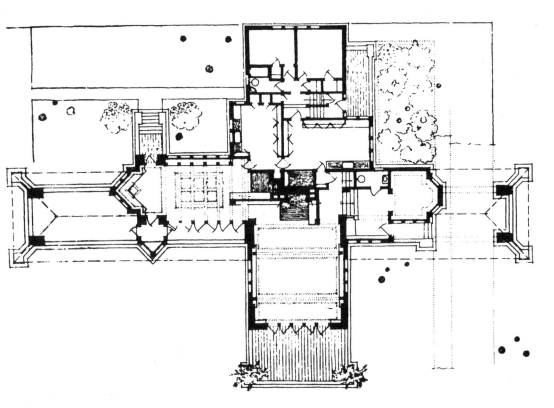

38.   Frank Lloyd Wright. Larkin Building, Buffalo, New York, 1904.

39.   Larkin Building. Interior.

40. *Frank Lloyd Wright. D.D. Martin House, Buffalo, New York, 1904. Living room.*

41. *Frank Lloyd Wright. Robie House, Chicago, Illinois, 1908–09.*

42. Robie House. Detail.

43. Parson Capen House, Topsfield, Massachusetts, 1683. Kitchen.

44. *Victor Horta. House, 4 Avenue Palmerson, Brussels, 1894. Interior.*

45. *Victor Horta. Maison du Peuple, Brussels, 1896–99. Auditorium.*

46. *Octopus vase. Minoan, 1600–1500 B.C.*

47. Antonio Gaudí. Casa Mila, Barcelona, 1905–10.

48. Vincent Van Gogh. "Starry Night," 1889. Oil on canvas. Collection, the Museum of Modern Art, New York.

49.   Casa Mila. Roof Detail.

50.   Eric Mendelsohn. Einstein Tower, Neubabelsberg, Germany, 1921.

51. *Auguste Perret. Garage,*
Rue de Ponthieu, Paris, 1905.

52. *Auguste Perret. Notre Dame, Le Raincy, 1922–23. Interior.*

53. *Auguste Perret. Place de l'Hotel de Ville, Le Havre, 1948–54.*

54. Otto Wagner. Post Office, Vienna, 1904–06. Interior

55. Adolf Loos. Steiner House, Vienna, 1910.

56. Peter Behrens. A.E.G. Turbine Factory, Berlin, 1909.

57. Walter Gropius and Hannes Meyer. Fagus Factory, Alfeld-an-der-Leine, 1910–14.

58. Fagus Factory. Interior detail.

59. *Walter Gropius. Model Factory, Werkbund Exhibition, Cologne, 1914.*

60. *Frank Lloyd Wright. City National Bank, Mason City, Iowa, 1909.*

61. *Model Factory. Façade with stair tower.*

62.   Frank Lloyd Wright. Ward Willits House, Highland Park, Illinois, 1900–02.

63.   Theo Van Doesburg. "Rhythm of a Russian Dance," 1918. Collection, the Museum of Modern Art, New York.

64.   George Vantongerloo. "Construction of Volume Relations," 1921. Mahogany. Collection, the Museum of Modern Art, New York.

65. Rietveld and Van Doesburg.
Project for a private house, 1920.

66. Gerrit Rietveld. Schröder House, Utrecht, 1924–25.

67. J. J. P. Oud. Café de Unie, Rotterdam, 1925.

68.   *Walter Gropius. Bauhaus, Dessau, 1925–26. Air view.*

69.   *Bauhaus. Studio Apartments.*

70.   *Bauhaus. Corner of workshop wing.*

71.   Mies van der Rohe. Project for a glass skyscraper, 1920–21.

72.   Mies van der Rohe. Project for a brick country house, 1923. Plan.

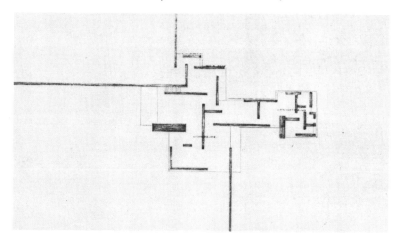

73.   *Project for a brick country house. Elevation.*

74.   *Mies van der Rohe. German Pavilion, International Exposition, Barcelona, 1929.*

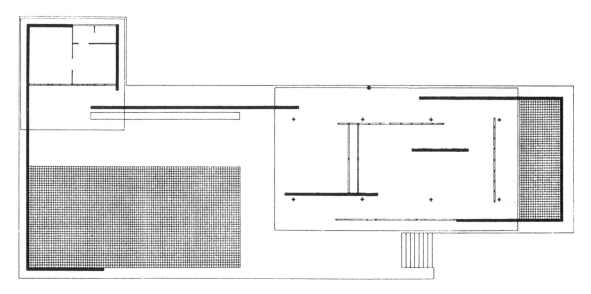

75. *Barcelona Pavilion. Plan.*

76. *Barcelona Pavilion. Sculpture by Kolbe.*

77.   *Barcelona Pavilion. View from end of court.*

78.   *Mies van der Rohe. Tugendhat House, Brno, Czechoslovakia, 1930.*

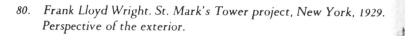

80. *Frank Lloyd Wright. St. Mark's Tower project, New York, 1929. Perspective of the exterior.*

79. *Frank Lloyd Wright. Barnsdall House, Los Angeles, California, 1920.*

81. *New York in 1953. Air view.*

82. Frank Lloyd Wright. Kaufmann House, "Falling Water," near Connellsville, Pennsylvania, 1936–37.

83. Frank Lloyd Wright. Goetsch-Winkler House, Okemos, Michigan, 1939. Court.

84.   Frank Lloyd Wright. Taliesin West, Phoenix, Arizona, 1938–59. Pool, house, and mountain.

85.   Taliesin West. Plan.

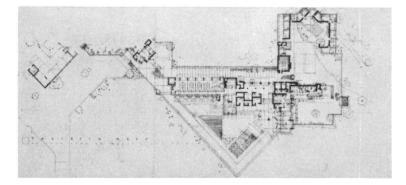

86.   Taliesin West. Loggia, desert, and mountain.

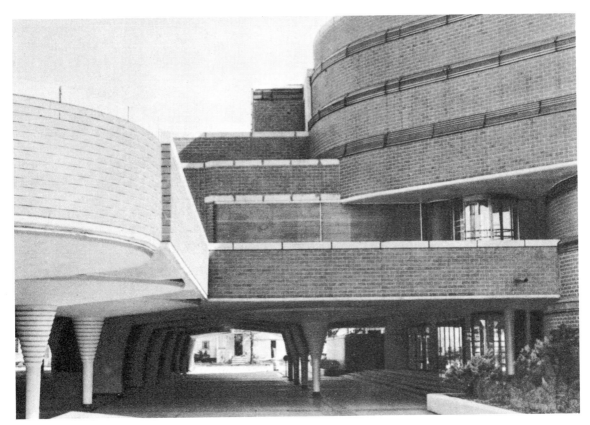

87.   *Frank Lloyd Wright. Johnson Wax Building, Racine, Wisconsin, 1936–39. Entrance.*

88.   *Johnson Wax Building. Interior.*

89. *Frank Lloyd Wright. Morris Gift Shop, San Francisco, California, 1948. Interior.*

90. *Guggenheim Museum, New York, 1946–59.*

91. *Guggenheim Museum. Interior.*

92. *Walter Gropius and the Architects' Collaborative. Harvard University Graduate Center, Cambridge, Massachusetts, 1948–50. Model.*

93. *Mies van der Rohe, Illinois Institute of Technology, 1940– . Model.*

94. *Illinois Institute of Technology compared with Vignola façades.*

95. *Illinois Institute of Technology. Alumni Memorial Hall.*

96. *Peter and Alison Smithson. Secondary School, Hunstanton, England, 1951–53.*

97. *Mies van der Rohe. Farnsworth House, Plano, Illinois, 1950 (designed earlier).*

98. *Mies van der Rohe. Apartment House,*
    860 Lake Shore Drive, Chicago, Illinois, 1951.

99. *Skidmore, Owings, and Merrill. Lever House,*
    New York, 1952.

100. *Mies van der Rohe and Philip Johnson.*
      Seagram Building, New York, 1958.

101. *Seagram Building. Detail.*

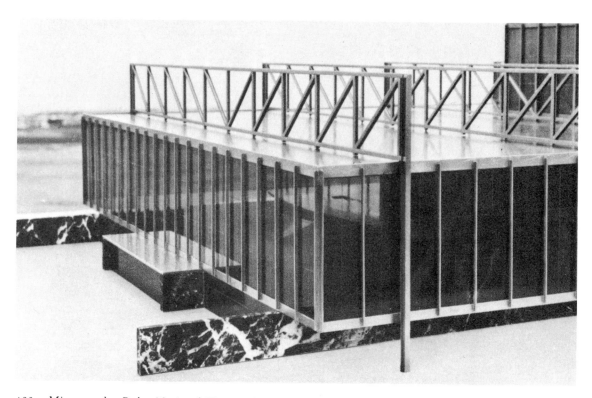

102. Mies van der Rohe. National Theater for Mannheim, Germany, 1953.   Model.

103. Mies van der Rohe. Cullinan Wing, Museum of Fine Arts, Houston, Texas, 1958–59.

103a. Philip Johnson. *Philip Johnson House, New Canaan, Connecticut, 1949. Living pavilion*

104.   Philip Johnson. *Munson-Williams-Proctor Institute, Utica, New York, 1957–60.*

105.   Philip Johnson. *First project for a Theater of the Dance, Lincoln Square, New York, 1959.*

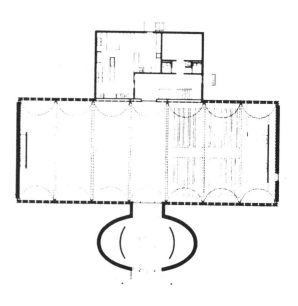

106. *Philip Johnson. Kneses Tifereth Israel*
Synagogue, Portchester, New York, 1954.

107. *Kneses Tifereth Israel Synagogue. Plan.*

108. *Kneses Tifereth Israel Synagogue. Interior.*

109. *Eero Saarinen. Kresge Auditorium, Massachusetts Institute of Technology, Cambridge, Massachusetts, 1955.*

110. *Edward Stone. United States Embassy, New Delhi, India, 1957–59.*

111. *Yamasaki, Leinweber, and Associates. McGregor Memorial Conference Center, Wayne University, Detroit, Michigan, 1957.*

112. *Skidmore, Owings, and Merrill. United States Air Force Academy, Colorado Springs, Colorado, 1955–58.*

113. *Alvar Aalto. Church, Vuoksenniska, Finland, 1956–58. Plan and section.*

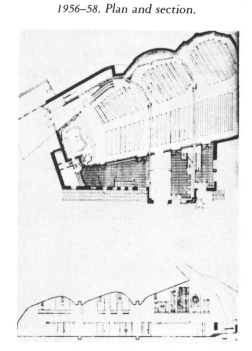

114. *Church, Vuoksenniska. Exterior detail.*

116. Alvar Aalto. Housing project, Munkkiniemi, Finland, 1938. Site plan.

115. Church, Vuoksenniska. Exterior.

117. Alvar Aalto. Civic Center, Säynätsalo, Finland, 1950–51. East entrance.

118. *Säynätsalo. Courtyard from the west.*

119. *Louis I. Kahn. Community Center, Trenton, New Jersey, 1955. Section and model.*

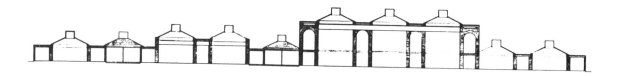

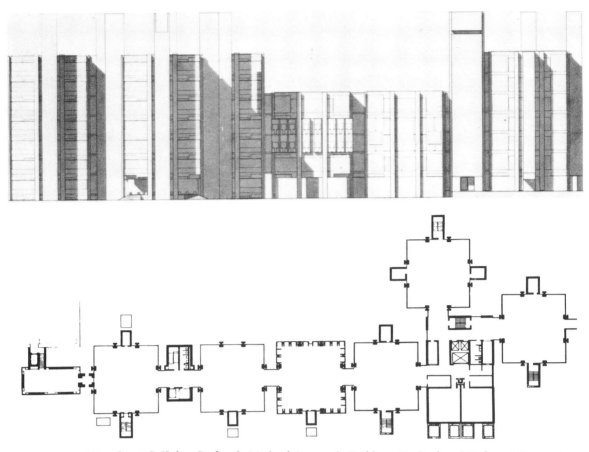

120. Louis I. Kahn. *Richards Medical Research Building, Medical and Biology Laboratories, University of Pennsylvania, Philadelphia, Pennsylvania, 1957–60. North elevation and plan.*

121. *Medical Laboratories. From the south.*

122. *Medical Laboratories. Entrance.*

123.   *The axis of the Acropolis with the Horns of Hymettos.*

124.   *Le Corbusier. Autostrade of "Une Ville Contemporaine," 1922.*

125.   *Le Corbusier. Ozenfant House, Paris, 1922. Studio.*

126. *Le Corbusier. Citrohan House on pilotis, Weissenhof Housing Exhibition, Stuttgart, 1927.*

127. *Le Corbusier. Swiss Dormitory, University City, Paris, 1930–32.*

128. Le Corbusier. Palace of the Soviets, 1931. Model.

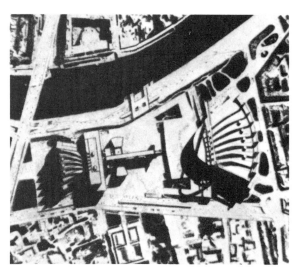

129. Palace of the Soviets. Model from above.

130. Le Corbusier. Union of the Cooperatives, Moscow, 1928–35. View of the model from above in 1930.

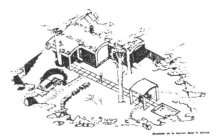

131. *Le Corbusier. Weekend House, suburbs of Paris, 1935. Isometric view.*

132. *Le Corbusier. Maison Jaoul, Neuilly, 1952.*

133. *Maison Jaoul. Interior.*

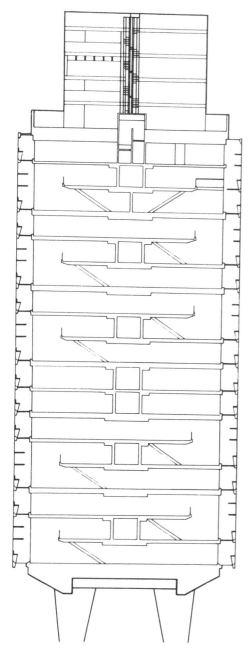

134. *Le Corbusier. Unité d'Habitation,*
Marseilles, 1946–52. Section.

135. *Unité d'Habitation.*

136. *Unité d'Habitation. Detail.*

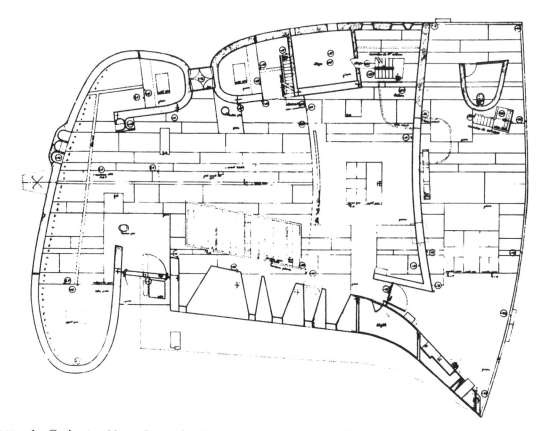

137.   Le Corbusier. Notre Dame du Haut, Ronchamp, 1951–55. Plan.

138.   Ronchamp. From the west.

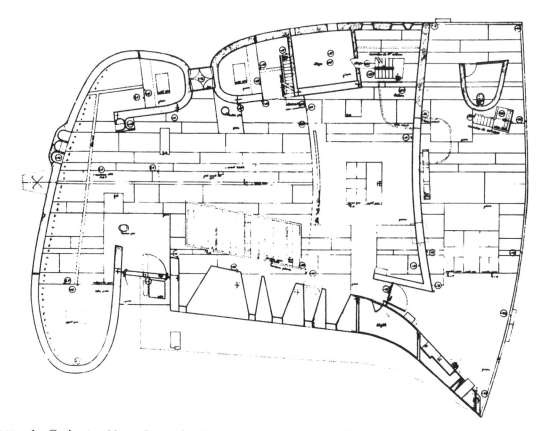

139. *Ronchamp. From the east.*

140. *Ronchamp. Interior, looking west.*

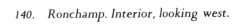

141. Ronchamp. From the south.

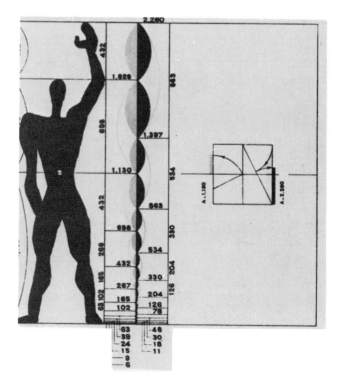

142. Le Corbusier. Le Modulor.

143. Le Corbusier. Monastery of La Tourette, Eveux, 1956–60

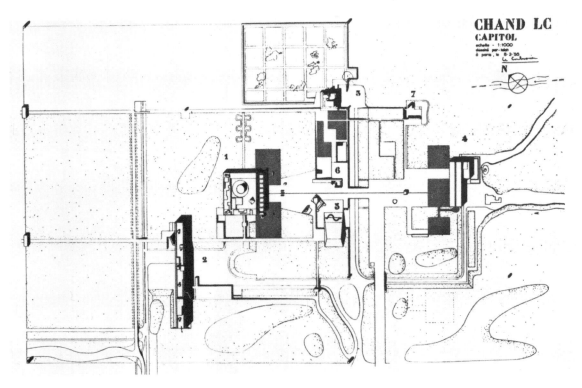

144. Le Corbusier. Chandigarh, India. Plan of the Capitol Buildings as of 1957.

145. Secretariat, Chandigarh, India, 1951–57. East façade.

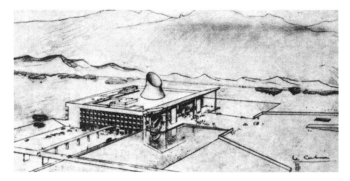

146. Assembly Building, Chandigarh. Perspective, 1955.

147. High Court Building, Chandigarh, 1951–56.

148. *High Court Building, Chandigarh. West façade, detail.*

150. *Paul Rudolph. High School, Sarasota, Florida, 1958–59. Perspective of entrance.*

149. *High Court Building, Chandigarh. Ramps.*

151. High Court, Chandigarh. The piers.

152. P. L. Troost. Deutsches Museum, Munich, 1938.

153. *Paul Rudolph. Art and Architecture Building, Yale University, 1961–63.*
154. *Government Center for New Haven, Connecticut. Redevelopment project, 1966.*

155. *Oak Street Connector, New Haven, Connecticut. As it looked in 1966.*
156. *Louis I. Kahn. Proposal for Center City, Philadelphia, project, 1956.*

157. *Louis I. Kahn. Unitarian Church,*
     Rochester, N.Y., 1961–63.
158. *Unitarian Church. Interior of the Main*
     Meeting Room.

160. *Venturi and Rauch. Guild House. Friends'*
     Housing for the Elderly, Philadelphia,
     1960–63.

159. *Louis I. Kahn. Indian Institute of*
     Management, Ahmedabad, 1964–66.
     Detail of arches.

161. *Louis H. Sullivan. National Farmers' Bank, Owatonna, Minnesota, 1907–08.*

163. *Karl Ehn. Heiligenstadt Houses. The Karl Marx Hof, Vienna, 1927.*

162. *Michel de Klerk. Housing built by the Public Utility Society, Amsterdam, 1918. View of Post Office and Apartments.*

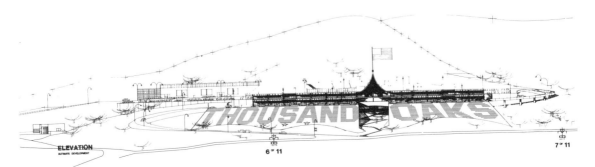

164. *Robert Venturi in association with Steven Izenour and Tony Pett, with the assistance of Denise Scott Brown. Urban Center for Thousand Oaks, California, 1969. Competition drawing.*

168. London County Council. Roehampton Housing Development, Richmond Park, London, 1959.

165. Schmid and Aichinger. Fuchsenfeldhof Houses, Vienna, 1924–25. Facades on the Platz in E Unit.

166. Charles Moore. Church Street South Public Housing, New Haven, Connecticut, 1966–72.

167. Emile Aillaud. La Grande Borne, Grigny, 1965–71.

169. Serafimov, Folger, and Kravetz. House of Industry, Kharkov, Soviet Union, 1924–1933.

171. Sheffield City Architects' Department. Park Hill Development, Sheffield, England, 1966. The Triple Pedestrian Bridge.

170. King's Dream of New York, The Cosmopolis of the Future, 1908.

172. Alexander Vesnin and Lubov Popova. Design for the Pageant "Battle and Victory," Petrograd, 1919–20.

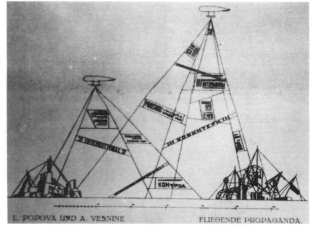

173. *Ivan Leonidov. Model of Project for Lenin Institute, 1927. View from the top.*

174. *Claes Oldenburg. Proposed Colossal Monument for the Thames River: Thames Ball, 1967.*

175. *Stirling and Gowan. Engineering Laboratory, Leicester University, Leicester, England, 1961–63.*

176. *Melnikov. Club House of City Working Men's Union, Moscow, 1927.*

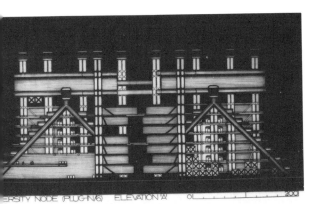

177. Peter Cook. Project for a New University, Living City Exposition, London, 1963. A Plug-In City.

179. Kenzo Tange. Yamanashi Communications Center, Kofu, Japan, 1966.

178. Roche, Dinkeloo and Associates. Coliseum, New Haven, Connecticut, 1967–72, with Knights of Columbus Building, 1967–69, at left.

180. Moshe Safdie. Habitat, Montreal, 1967.

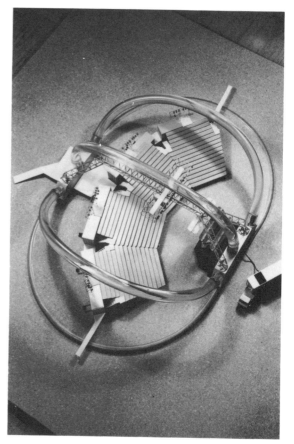

181. Airstream caravans in wagon-train circle for the night. 1970.
182. De Bretteville, Hodgetts, and Kupper. Design for a Mobile Theater, 1971.

183. Venturi and Rauch. Fire Station #4, Columbus, Indiana, 1965–67.
184. Robert Venturi and John Rauch with the assistance of Terry Vaughan. Trubek and Wislocki Houses, Nantucket, Massachusetts, 1971–1972.

BIBLIOGRAPHICAL NOTE

Since a certain amount of bibliography has already been indicated, this note will deal only with a few general studies of modern architecture, and of major periods and movements within it, in which major points of view are enunciated and more specialized bibliographies can be found. The most detailed study of the architecture of the nineteenth and twentieth centuries has been carried on by Henry-Russell Hitchcock. His earliest work, *Modern Architecture, Romanticism and Reintegration* (New York, 1929), was the first serious attempt to establish the contours of the modern period so far as its architectural history was concerned. His next book, written with Philip Johnson for an important exhibition at the Museum of Modern Art in New York, focused upon the nineteen-twenties and established the basic formal definition of the new European architecture of that period, naming it as well *(The International Style: Architecture since 1922,* New York, 1932). J. M. Richards' popular paperback, *An Introduction to Modern Architecture* (Harmondsworth, 1940), took its basic points of view from the afore-mentioned, highly perceptive volumes, as many other books have also done. Numerous later publications by Hitchcock, including basic books on Richardson and Wright, were followed by his attempt to describe the formation of mid-nineteenth-century "Victorian" design: *Early Victorian Architecture in Britain* (2 vol., New Haven and London, 1954). Finally, his Pelican volume presented what was in effect a handbook for the modern period as a whole: *Architecture Nineteenth and Twentieth Centuries* (Harmondsworth and Baltimore, 1958). This includes a usefully selected bibliography, arranged by century, by country, and by architect.

Hitchcock's work, tending as it has done towards the encyclopedic chronicle, has not had a general popular influence comparable to that of Sigfried Giedion's more personal and synoptic method, as demonstrated in his *Space, Time and Architecture*, first published in Cambridge, Massachusetts, in 1941, and since reprinted and re-edited many times. The latter work, enthusiastically conceived and brilliant in its intuitive analogies, was especially influential among architects during the nineteen-forties and the early fifties. This may have been the case because it gave them an emotionally persuasive combination of everything architectural students seemed to want during those years: a heartening relation to science in the "space-time" analogy, myths and martyrs for the modern movement, lonely culture heroes, themselves, attempting to bring about the "integration" of society according to the rather special principles of the C.I.A.M. (International Congresses of Modern Architecture) group. Most striking of all was Giedion's uprooting of the modern architect from his true ancestry in the revolutionary architecture of the later eighteenth century. In this way the whole scope, meaning, and inner development of modern architecture were distorted, and a miscegenetic ancestry, joining the nineteenth-century engineers with the architects of the Baroque, had to be arranged. It was as if modern man were more or less consciously attempting to conceal his true character from himself. This seems especially evident in view of the fact that Giedion had already made a study of Romantic-Classicism and was indeed the first historian to use this extremely useful term (*Spätbarocker und romantischer Klassizismus*, Munich, 1922). Moreover, Emil Kaufmann had clearly indicated the germinal relationship between the experiments of the later eighteenth century and the architecture of the twentieth, in his *Von Ledoux bis Le Corbusier, Ursprung und Entwicklung der Autonome Architektur* (Vienna and Leipzig, 1933). Kaufmann then went on to analyze the architecture of the Enlightenment and the Revolution in more detail, and to demonstrate its decisive break with the Baroque and its importance for later development (*Idem* "Three Revolutionary Architects, Boullée, Ledoux, and Lequeu," trans., *American Philosophical Society*, 42, pt. 3, 1952, pp. 476–547. Also, *Architecture in the Age of Reason*, Cambridge, Massachusetts, 1955).

A vociferous campaign to counteract the influence of Giedion has been carried on by Bruno Zevi, but here a restrictive intention has been equally evident, since Zevi's insistence upon the superiority of an "organic" approach deriving from Wright's over a "rationalistic" method typified by Le Corbusier has resulted in its own kind of historical confusion (*Towards an Organic Architecture*, London, 1950. Also, *Storia dell'Architettura Moderna*, Turin, 1950). Zevi's point of view seems essentially that of the spatially continuous phase of modern architecture, apparently reinforced by his own almost archetypally Italic preoccupation with spatial engulfment (*Architecture as Space*, New York, 1957, trans. by Milton Gendel; originally *Saper vedere l'Architettura*, 4th edition, Turin 1953). However, Zevi's book, *Poetica dell'Architettura Neoplastica* (Milan, 1953), seems of special interest at the present time. Many other works might be cited, from Nikolaus Pevsner's *Pioneers of the Modern Movement* (London, 1936), reissued as *Pioneers of Modern Design* (London, 1949), to Ian McCallum's *Architecture, U.S.A.* (New York, 1959), and Jurgen Joedicke's *A History of Modern Architecture* (trans., New York, 1959). Most recent of all are Reyner Banham's close review of the European architecture of the early twentieth century in terms of its theoretical texts, projects, and buildings (*Theory and Design in the First Machine Age*, London, 1960), and Peter Blake's *The Master Builders* (New York, 1960). Banham's book is of considerable historical interest, and we should not be put off by its unnecessarily technocratic conclusions.

My own belief, indicated by my publications cited in the notes, is that the meaning of modern architecture can be properly understood only in the light of all the architectures ever conceived by man, and that it can hardly be written about without reference to one or another of those architectures. I do not suggest that Jung's concept of a "collective unconscious" should be thought to apply here. It is true that when similar themes are handled, many unconscious parallels will appear. At the same time, the most creative architects since the later eighteenth century, with the whole past open to them, have consciously dealt with the problems of existence, and thus of expression, through their view of history and their consequent sense of personal mission as modern men. Indeed, the greatest of them, such as Wright and Le Corbusier, have been doubly conscious of the layer upon layer of meaning implicit in their sources of inspiration, and of the timeless implications of their large, few, and simple themes.

NOTES

1. Cf. Emil Kaufmann, *Architecture in the Age of Reason*, Cambridge, Mass., 1955, p. 87.
2. Especially Sigfried Giedion, *Space, Time and Architecture*, Cambridge, Mass., 1943, pp. 41–95.
3. Rudolf Wittkower, *Art and Architecture in Italy, 1600–1750*, Baltimore, 1958, pp. 236–37.
4. Focillon best understood the revolutionary nature of Piranesi's vision: "une architecture à la fois impossible et réelle." Henri Focillon, *Giovanni Battista Piranesi*, Paris, 1928, p. 190.
5. Henry Adams, *The Education of Henry Adams*, Washington, 1907, especially Chapter XXV, "The Dynamo and the Virgin," pp. 331–40. An architectural experience apparently had much to do with Adams' perception of the revolutionary character of the machine age. ". . . he found himself lying in the Gallery of Machines at the Great Exposition of 1900, with his historical neck broken by the sudden irruption of force totally new," p. 334.
6. The term "Romantic-Classicism" was first used by Sigfried Giedion, *Spätbarocker und romantischer Klassizismus*, Munich, 1922. The term "Romantic-Naturalism" is my own and is intended to serve as a better balance to Romantic-Classicism than does the term "Picturesque," which might also be used for it—and was used in the period. But certain "picturesque" attitudes also infuse the Romantic-Classic itself to some extent, and the term might, therefore, be better left aside for the moment. Cf. C. Hussey, *The Picturesque*, London, 1927; and D. Pilcher, *The Regency Style, 1800 to 1830*, London, 1947.
7. For example, the decided curvatures of the Parthenon and other temples were not noticed, unbelievably enough, until well into the nineteenth century. Stuart and Revett, *Antiquities of Athens*, London, 1762, drew all the lines straight.
8. The most determined attempt to read modern architectural history in this way was made by Emil Kaufmann, although he would not allow Ledoux to be grouped with the romantic-classicists. Kaufmann, *Von Ledoux bis Le Corbusier; Ursprung und Entwicklung der Autonome Architektur*, Vienna and Leipzig, 1933.
9. As in the so-called "Bay Region Style." Zevi regards the later stages of this romantic-naturalist movement as of outstanding importance. Cf. Bruno Zevi, *Towards an Organic Architecture*, London, 1950; and *Storia dell'Architettura Moderna*, Turin, 1950.
10. The terms were first paired by C. L. V. Meeks, "Picturesque Eclecticism," *Art Bulletin*, XXXII, 1950, pp. 226–35.
11. The fullest account of the Victorian amalgam is H.-R. Hitchcock, *Early Victorian Architecture in Britain*, 2 vols., New Haven and London, 1954.
12. The *Ecclesiologist*, beginning publication in 1841, used "truth" and

"reality" as its key critical words. For Butterfield, see J. N. Summerson, "William Butterfield," *Architectural Review*, December, 1945, pp. 166–75. For Viollet-le-Duc, see P. Gant, *Viollet-le-Duc, sa vie, son œuvre, sa doctrine*, Paris, 1914.

13. This concept is explored in terms of political philosophy by Albert Camus, *L'Homme Révolté*, Paris, 1951. For its relationship to architectural thought, see Donald Drew Egbert, "The Idea of Organic Expressionism and American Architecture," in *Evolutionary Thought in America*, ed. Stowe Persons, New Haven, 1950, pp. 336–96.

14. Lawrence saw it as an intrinsically American urge to "get away." D. H. Lawrence, *Studies in Classic American Literature*, London, 1922; Doubleday Anchor edition, New York, 1955, pp. 13 ff.

15. I have tried to explore the American predilection for the linear screen in "The Precisionist Strain in American Architecture," *Art in America*, No. 3, 1960, pp. 46–53.

16. For the formal and theoretical development of American domestic architecture in wood during this period, see my "Romantic-Rationalism and the Expression of Structure in Wood: Downing, Wheeler, Gardner and the 'Stick Style,' " *Art Bulletin*, XXXV, 1953, pp. 121–42.

17. These developments and their relationship to Richard Norman Shaw's English "Queen Anne" and the American colonial revival are discussed in detail in my *The Shingle Style, Architectural Theory and Design from Richardson to the Origins of Wright*, New Haven, 1955.

18. Louis Sullivan, *Kindergarten Chats*, revised 1918, New York, 1947, pp. 29–30.

19. Geoffrey Scott, *The Architecture of Humanism, A Study in the History of Taste*, New York, 1914, esp. pp. 210–47. In this connection, see also my "Louis Sullivan's Architectural Ornament, a Brief Note Concerning Humanist Design in the Age of Force," *Perspecta, The Yale Architectural Journal*, 5, 1959, pp. 73–80.

20. Wright's own first house of 1889 was closely based upon published designs by Bruce Price at Tuxedo Park: the Kent House, reproduced here, and the Chandler House. Cf. *The Shingle Style*, figs. 108, 109, 155, 156.

21. As in the Kent House. For a discussion of the cross-axial plan and its antecedents see my *Frank Lloyd Wright*, New York, 1960, pp. 17–18, figs. 5, 18, 20, 21, 22, and note 21.

22. See Frank Lloyd Wright, *An Autobiography*, New York, 1943, pp. 139–50. Also my *Frank Lloyd Wright*, pp. 17–18, for the analogies to mass democracy.

23. Giedion insists that Cubist painting and the later European architectural development after it were based upon "another spatial conception" than Wright's, one which he calls "Space-Time." *Space, Time and Architecture*, p. 348 and pp. 367–82. It is difficult to accept either the defining term or the distinction. Picasso and Braque fragmented solids and brought the resultant planes into a continuously sliding spatial relationship, exactly as Wright was doing in the same years, c. 1906–14. Their painting is indeed much closer to Wright's work than it is to most of the European architecture of the teens and twenties, as is indicated below. And the space-time formula in physics involves such enormous

velocities that, in effect, all objects become one—as Meyer Schapiro has pointed out in lectures. But the Cubists and Wright were tearing all objects to pieces and rearranging the fragments. Curiously, the "space-time" analogy, though unsatisfactory in any case, would actually apply better to the continuously curving lines of *Art Nouveau*, also discussed below, which, despite his liking for Horta, Giedion sees as an " 'anti' movement" of comparatively little importance. *Op. cit.*, p. 237.

24. Cf. S. T. Madsen, *The Sources of Art Nouveau*, Oslo and New York, 1956. For the association of its Celtic interlace with Sullivan's ornament, see my article cited note 19 above, figs. 2, 5, 8–10. Significantly enough, James Joyce—whose own work, cited at the head of this part, carried the principles of fragmentation and continuity farther than any other writer has done—asserted that he had studied the illuminations of the *Book of Kells* and that his own method of composition derived from them, or (once in *Finnegans Wake*, p. 122) vice versa. (Richard Ellmann, *James Joyce*, New York, 1959, pp. 558-59.)

25. Herakleitos, fragments 41–42, as in Arthur Fairbanks, ed. and trans., *The First Philosophers of Greece*, New York, 1898, p. 35.

26. Fragments of Minoan and Mycenaean art were being widely published during the second half of the nineteenth century, especially from 1878 onward. Knossos publication began in 1901. Cf. Sir Arthur J. Evans, *The Palace of Minos at Knossos*, 4 vols. and index in 7 vols., London, 1921–36.

27. Cf. George R. Collins, *Antonio Gaudí*, New York, 1960, *passim*.

28. For an extremely, perhaps overly, sympathetic study of Perret's concrete aesthetic, see Peter Collins, *Concrete, the Vision of a New Architecture; a Study of Auguste Perret and His Precursors* (London, 1959).

29. Cf. Reyner Banham, "Ornament and Crime, The Decisive Contribution of Adolf Loos," *Architectural Review*, February, 1957, pp. 85–88.

30. Cf. my "Frank Lloyd Wright vs. The International Style," *Art News*, LIII, March, 1954, pp. 32 ff.; also *Art News*, LIII, September, 1954, pp. 48–49. Also, my *Frank Lloyd Wright*, pp. 23–24, 26–27.

31. Cf. Bruno Zevi, *Poetica dell'Architettura Neoplastica*, Milan, 1953.

32. Gropius and his followers have always disliked admitting the debt the Bauhaus owed *de Stijl*, probably because of the "functional" and "moral" justification they claimed for their forms. They therefore sought to conceal—most disastrously of all, from themselves—the rather arbitrary, certainly "formalistic," process through which they had actually evolved. Cf. Walter Gropius, *The New Architecture and the Bauhaus*, trans. by P. Morton Shand, New York and London, 1937. Also, *Bauhaus, 1914–28*, ed. by Herbert Bayer, Boston, 1959. For the period as a whole: Alfred H. Barr, Jr., *Cubism and Abstract Art*, Museum of Modern Art, New York, 1936.

33. For Mies' work see Philip Johnson, *Mies Van der Rohe*, new ed., New York, 1953, and Arthur Drexler, *Mies Van der Rohe*, New York, 1960.

34. Cf. D. T. Tselos, "Exotic Influences in the Architecture of Frank Lloyd Wright," *Magazine of Art*, XLVI, April, 1953, pp. 160–69. Also, my *Frank Lloyd Wright*, p. 24, figs. 59–69.

35. Hugh Ferris, *The Metropolis of Tomorrow*, New York, 1929; *idem*,

Power in Buildings, New York, 1953. Even Raymond Hood's more superficially "modern" skyscrapers of the early 30's are still involved in these categories: The Daily News Building of 1930, a vertically insistent, compressed slab, like those which were to form his and Harrison's Rockefeller Center; The McGraw-Hill Building of 1931, with horizontal window bands, defined as a symmetrically stepped, triangular mass. These make even more remarkable the inventive achievement of George Howe and William Lescaze in their Philadelphia Savings Fund Society Building of 1930–32. Here a neutrally cladded service tower is articulated from the main office tower of vertically continuous columns and cantilevered floor slabs. Cf. *Cahiers d'Art*, Vol. XXVIII, 1933, p. 237.

36. In my *Frank Lloyd Wright*, pp. 28 ff., figs. 96, 97, 102–03. My forthcoming book, *The Earth, The Temple, and The Gods*, scheduled for publication in 1961, attempts to explore the Minoan and Greek use of landscape forms. Wright later actually built his own sacred horned mountain in the Beth Sholom Synagogue, Elkins Park, Pennsylvania, of 1959. This would appear to have been closely based upon the Cone of Astarte in her horned enclosure at Byblos, as published by Evans in 1901. *Frank Lloyd Wright*, pp. 31–32, figs. 125–26.

37. *Ibid.*, pp. 29–30, figs. 104–20, 127. See also note 59 below.

38. See my "Archetype and Order in Recent American Architecture," *Art in America*, December, 1954, pp. 251–61.

39. Rudolf Wittkower, *Architectural Principles in the Age of Humanism*, London, 1949.

40. The recently completed Pirelli Tower in Milan by Gio Ponti, Pier Luigi Nervi, and others, is of course the exact opposite, using bearing walls with cantilevered floor slabs. It thus becomes a faceted tower of vertical planes. Cf. *Architectural Review*, January, 1960.

41. Johnson's attempts to work out various kinds of column screens, like those of Greek stoas, are striking in this regard, as is a whole gamut of special effects by Saarinen, ranging from the structural bravura of the Yale Hockey Rink to the Mannerist ambiguity of wall plane and fenestration in the Oslo and London Embassies, and from the flapping wings in concrete of the Idlewild Terminal to the rather effective Gothic stage design of his new colleges for Yale. Cf. William H. Jordy, "The Mies-less Johnson," *Architectural Forum*, CXI, 3, September, 1959, pp. 114–23; and Lawrence Lessing, "The Diversity of Eero Saarinen," *Architectural Forum*, CXIII, 1, July, 1960, pp. 94–103. Yet, these two architects, by whom some of the most important buildings of the next few years will be built, are too dissimilar to be lightly bracketed together. Johnson at his best is admirably lucid, unsentimental, and abstract, with the most ruthlessly aristocratic, highly studied taste of anyone practicing in America today. All that nervous sensibility, lively intelligence, and a stored mind can do, he does. One must take him as he is. Saarinen, on the other hand, seeks earnestly and perennially to produce a ready and communicable symbolic form for each project in hand, and the impression persists that, like Wright in his old age, Saarinen in his middle years is building his sketches. One waits, with some optimism, the time when the process will advance beyond literary solecism to

perceptions more wholly architectural and symbols more integral and considered.

42. For this reason, the hopeful tone of the article cited note 38 above had changed by 1960, when the rapid stultification of the movement had become inescapably apparent. Cf. William H. Jordy, "The Formal Image, U.S.A.," *Architectural Review*, March, 1960, pp. 157–65.

43. As discussed in the article cited note 15 above.

44. For Aalto see Frederick A. Gutheim, *Alvar Aalto*, New York, 1960. Also, Joedicke has recently pointed out that Aalto's later work has an ancestor in the design of Hugo Haering, who opposed the general movement toward arbitrarily pure geometry that took place in architecture during the twenties. Haering's Garkau Farm, near Lübeck, of 1923–24, does indeed remind us of such late buildings by Aalto as those at Vuoksenniska and Säynätsalo, discussed below. Jurgen Joedicke, "Haering at Garkau," *Architectural Review*, May, 1960, pp. 313–18.

45. Kahn's career has probably been the most unusual of any contemporary architect's, in so far as its maturity came so late. Kahn was born in Estonia in 1901 and brought to Philadelphia as a child. There, as he has said, he derived his education from the Public Library, the Museum, and the University of Pennsylvania. (Once, asked to define a city, he replied: "A city is a place where a small boy, as he walks through it, may see something that will tell him what he wants to do his whole life.") Kahn's opportunities for building were delayed by depression, war, and his own integrity, but the long years of waiting apparently resulted in a richer intellectual and emotional experience than most architects, successful in youth, have been able to assimilate. (Of his trip to Pisa he wrote: "When I first came to Pisa I went straight in the direction of the Piazza. Nearing it and seeing a distant glimpse of the Tower filled me so that I stopped short to enter a shop where I bought an ill-fitting English jacket. Not daring to enter the Piazza I diverted to other streets toward it but never allowing myself to arrive. The next day I went straight for the Tower, touched its marble, and that of the Duomo and Baptistry. The next day I boldly entered the buildings." Of his trip to Paestum he was moved to say: "Reflect on the great event in architecture when the walls parted and columns became." He also wrote: "What a column is in steel or concrete is not yet felt as part of us.") The first of Kahn's mature buildings was the new Art Gallery for Yale University, designed when he was fifty-two years of age. He now has many commissions, and a monograph should be written about his work. So far, his projects have been best published, appropriately enough, by the architectural students of Yale University, to whom he gave so much as a teacher. *Perspecta, The Yale Architectural Journal*, 2, 1953, pp. 11–27; 3, 1955, pp. 47–63; 4, 1957, pp. 2–3, 58–65. Recently, *Architectural Forum*, CXIII, 1, July, 1960, pp. 82 ff.

46. For Smithson's later work see *Architectural Review*, September, 1957, and May, 1960; for Stirling's, *Architectural Review*, April, 1958, and, for his flats at Ham Common, October, 1958. Stirling has said that Le Corbusier's Maisons Jaoul, discussed below, recalled the vernacular buildings of his native Liverpool. *Perspecta*, 6, 1960, pp. 88–97.

47. Le Corbusier's influence has been felt around the world. Partly because of this, it has seemed appropriate to exclude from so necessarily compressed a study as this the architectures of many areas which most closely derive from it, such as Latin America and Japan. Cf. Philip Goodwin and G. E. Kidder Smith, *Brazil Builds*, New York, 1943; and H.-R. Hitchcock, *Latin American Architecture Since 1945*, New York, 1955. The Japanese work in concrete by Tange should also be noted. Cf. *Architectural Record*, July, 1958, pp. 127–38. See also G. E. Kidder Smith, *Italy Builds*, London, 1955.

48. Le Corbusier's own buildings and projects have been exhaustively published by the architect himself in the many volumes of his *Oeuvre Complète*, which document his career from 1910 to the present. The synoptic critical study which it deserves has, however, not yet been written.

49. As in the writings of the Existentialists, especially those of Sartre. The author has been told by colleagues of Le Corbusier that he is not interested in Existentialism as a philosophy or informed about it. This does not prevent the parallel between his work and Sartre's from being a fundamental one. In his architect's sense of the relevance of nature, however, Le Corbusier is closer at once to Greek thought and to that of Camus, as cited at the beginning of this book.

50. The comments about Greek temples and siting made here and below derive from my forthcoming book cited note 36 above.

51. Le Corbusier (Charles-Edouard Jeanneret), *Vers une Architecture*, Paris, 1923; trans. by Frederick Etchells as *Towards a New Architecture*, London, 1927, pp. 173, 188.

52. *Ibid.*, pp. 190, 193.

53. In this the influence of the Italian "Futurists" of 1910–14, beloved by Banham (see Bibliographical Note), may legitimately be assumed. But Le Corbusier lived in a time with more dimension and was more Mediterranean than they. So he reproduced one of his most quoted aphorisms under a photograph of the "Empress of Asia": "Architecture is the masterly, correct and magnificent play of masses brought together in light." *Ibid.*, pp. 31, 95.

54. *Ibid.*, pp. 222–23.

55. Le Corbusier first raised his Citrohan House on columns in 1922, and the project bears certain resemblances to Wright's concrete-block Millard House, of 1923. Cf. my *Frank Lloyd Wright*, plates 64, 65.

56. In this it should be contrasted with the compressed slab on slender columns of the Ministry of Education and Public Health in Rio de Janeiro, of 1937–42, where the *brise-soleil* of Le Corbusier's earlier Algerian projects was first used by Niemeyer and Costa as a thin, linear, and painterly surface element—something like the same architects' pierced screens which have had such an effect upon Stone. Cf. Henry-Russell Hitchcock, *Architecture, Nineteenth and Twentieth Centuries*, Harmondsworth and Baltimore, 1958, figs. 171, 187. Similarly the alternately flaccid and brittle character of Niemeyer's monumental buildings for Costa's Brasilia should now be contrasted with Le Corbusier's forms at Chandigarh, discussed below. For Brasilia, cf. Stamo Papadaki, *Oscar Niemeyer*, New York, 1960, fig. 7 and plates 19–25, 30, 38, 83–90.

57. Geoffrey Scott, *op. cit.*, New York, 1914, p. 239.

58. *Ibid.*, same page. It is true that Scott would probably not have approved of Le Corbusier or of Sullivan either. His own buildings, hardly up to his splendid writing, were apparently more or less "Georgian" in derivation.

59. Le Corbusier had also studied the non-Hellenic aspects of the Mediterranean tradition. He indeed published a drawing of one of the goddess sanctuaries on Malta in his review, *L'Esprit Nouveau*, in the twenties. Stirling also finds close prototypes for the chapels in the peasant houses of Ischia. *Perspecta*, 6, 1960, p. 89. Cf. Guido F. von Kaschnitz-Weinberg, *Die Mittelmeerischen Grundlagen der Antiken Kunst*, Frankfurt am Main, 1944, esp. figs. 36, 37, 39. Also, Gertrude R. Levy, *The Gate of Horn*, London, 1948, plates. 15, 16b; figs. 62a, b.

60. I attempted to distinguish "classic" from "classicizing" art and to examine the relationship of the former to modern work (especially that of Picasso and Le Corbusier) in a talk given at the joint meeting of the American Archaeological Association and the American Philological Society in Philadelphia, December, 1956: "The Nature of the Classical in Art," *Yale French Studies*, nos. 19 and 20, 1958, pp. 107–24. Also, certain references to Indian architecture may perhaps be found in Chandigarh: in the plan and in the parasols of High Court and projected Governor's Palace. On the other hand, the whole parti and the character of the forms themselves clearly grow out of Le Corbusier's own pre-Indian development.

61. Rudolph was thus in the grip of the American "precisionism" I referred to earlier. See note 15 above. His more recent project, for the Yale School of Art and Architecture, still inspired by Le Corbusier's work, is rather more integral and stronger, as are various projects which derive more directly from the Maisons Jaoul. For the reasons indicated earlier, it has always been extremely difficult for Americans to conceive of themselves as taking position in space with humanistic confidence. This, as has also been mentioned before, makes Sullivan's and Richardson's achievements all the more remarkable. A contrast between American and European portraiture—whether between Copley and Reynolds, or between Eakins and Courbet—can elucidate the problem. The forthcoming study of American painting by John McCoubrey will undoubtedly explore these and related questions.

*A few general books not cited in the following notes (62–98), which deserve
special mention are:*
Leonardo Benevolo, Storia dell'Architettura Moderna, *Bari, 1960 (solid
contemporary Giedionesque-sociological); Peter Collins,* Changing Ideals
in Modern Architecture, 1750–1950, *London, 1965 (good old-fashioned
Academic); and* Landscapes: selected writings of J. B. Jackson, *ed. by Ervin
H. Zube, Amherst, Mass., 1970 (brilliant human geography, a new approach).*

62. Discussed in my "Art and Architecture Building, Yale University,"
Architectural Review, 135 (1964), pp. 325–332, I regret whatever repeti-
tion in subject matter may occur in this text with my *American Architecture and Urbanism*, New York, 1969. As stated above, the character
of the decade on an international level seems to me to make such treat-
ment unavoidable. Interpretive generalizations can, however, be made
much more confidently now than in 1969, especially with the help of the
international data. I also regret the necessary omission here of illustrations of the whole lively Latin American development from Cuba to
Tierra del Fuego during the past decade, but the reader is referred to
its most recent general coverage by the brave and devoted teacher and
architect, Francisco Bullrich, of Argentina *(New Directions in Latin
American Architecture*, New York, 1969).

63. Cf. George L. Hersey, *High Victorian Gothic: A Study in Associa-
tionism*, Baltimore, 1972, pp. xviii–xix, 53–60. In this connection one
thinks especially of the work of William Butterfield, pp. 114–124; and
see also Paul Thompson, *William Butterfield*, London, 1971.

64. For Mailer's remarks and my reply see *Architectural Forum, 120* (April,
1964), pp. 96–97. As I indicated there, I think that Mailer was right in
many ways in his view of contemporary modern architecture as at least
prototypatotalitarian. Some of it has since become much more so. For my
reaction to Redevelopment, dating from 1966, see "The Threat and the
Promise of Urban Redevelopment in New Haven," *Zodiac, 17* (1967),
pp. 171–176, and Letter to the Editor, *Journal of the American Institute
of Planners, 34* (March, 1968), p. 129.

65. For a fuller account of New Haven and "cataclysmic" Redevelopment,
see my *American Architecture and Urbanism*, esp. pp. 245–255. For
America since 1945 in general, pp. 178–245. Recently, for Le Corbusier's
planning see Norma Evenson, *Chandigarh*, Berkeley, 1966; and *Idem,
Le Corbusier: The Machine and the Grand Design*, New York, 1969.

66. For Kahn's general development, his Beaux-Arts training, and his
theory of Form and Design, see my *Louis I. Kahn*, New York, 1962
(which should now be brought up to date with Kahn's magnificent
production of the sixties and seventies), and "Light, Form, and Power:
New Work of Louis Kahn," *Architectural Forum, 121* (August–September 1964), pp. 162–170; and from the splendid show by Arthur
Drexler and others at the Museum of Modern Art in 1966, with comments and captions by me, "Recent Work of Louis Kahn," *Zodiac,
17* (1967), pp. 58–118.

67. As expected in the first edition of this book (above, p. 44), it was indeed
the concrete and brick or block structure of the New Brutalism, so-called,

which formed the basic vernacular of the sixties, perhaps tending to wane toward 1970. For the term and his assessment of the movement see Reyner Banham, *The New Brutalism: Ethic or Aesthetic?*, New York, 1966.

68. For example, the Abstract Expressionism of the fifties was idealistic, the Pop Art of the early sixties ironic; and most later movements in the visual arts and literature alike have been touched by the ironic spirit in various ways. Early in the decade I tried to trace its presence in architecture: "L'Ironie en Architecture," *Revue d'Esthétique*, 15 (1962), pp. 245–253, and later: *American Architecture and Urbanism*, pp. 230 ff.

69. For semeiology in architecture, though developed in rather more elaborate terms of Levi Straussian structural analysis than seem to me necessary for an understanding of the operative meaning here, which is of the building as a signpost telling the observer what it is about, see Alan Colquhon, "Typology and Design Method," *Arena* (June, 1967), pp. 11–14, reprinted in Charles Jencks and George Baird, eds., *Meaning in Architecture*, New York, 1970. The ideas advanced in that anthology of critical opinion are related to various aspects of the theoretical and experimental developments in England discussed below, and a number of them have been sympathetically cited by Venturi as well, as in Robert Venturi, Denise Scott Brown, and Steven Izenour, *Learning from Las Vegas*, Cambridge, Massachusetts, 1972, especially pp. 88–90.

70. Robert Venturi, *Complexity and Contradiction in Architecture*, New York, 1966. This presents Venturi's critical philosophy and his early works. The vicious reaction of many architects to that philosophy and those works, unparalleled in the profession for sheer nastiness since the reception of Le Corbusier's *Vers une Architecture*, of 1923, are the best indication of their innovative significance. The symbolic television aerial of the Guild House came under special attack. The "idealistic" view of the fifties simply could not accept it. One could not make architecture out of things people really weren't supposed to do, like look at television. The aerial is thus "realistic" but also, as Le Corbusier's details and appliances often were, at least partly ironic. At the same time, the upward lift of Venturi's facade needed a crowning element. What was it to be? From that point of view the aerial makes considerable visual no less than iconographic sense. In my opinion, Venturi is a brilliantly gifted and entirely traditional, visually-oriented architect who has simply been able to open his eyes to what "is" instead of what he or others think "ought to be." Since the former is usually, and not surprisingly, richer and more interesting than the latter, his work has acquired a special vitality, freshness, and poignancy.   *145*

71. *American Architecture and Urbanism*, pp. 126–129.

72. In the revival of appreciation for the traditional street as a valuable environment no book has been more important than that of Jane Jacobs, *The Death and Life of Great American Cities*, New York, 1961. Still, I think experience has shown that once the old street has been bombed out by Redevelopment it can never be realistically recreated. Instead, other presently more viable ways to encourage similar values of multiple

use, intimate scale, excitement, and human interaction must be found. Hence: Aillaud, Moore, and so on, discussed below, creating as it were synonyms for the street and the square.

73. Cf. Helen Searing, "Eigen Haard: Workers' Housing and the Amsterdam School," *Architectura, 2* (1971), pp. 148–175.

74. The social history and the statistics are well known, as in Erwin Schmidt, *Wiener Stadtgeschichte*, Vienna-Munich, 1968, pp. 90–91. Many of these programs continued along lines of advance initiated in the 1890s by the Christian Democrats under Karl Lueger. See in general: Felix Czeike, *Liberale, christlichsoziale und sozialdemokratische Kommunalpolitik (1861–1934), dargestellt am Beispiel der Gemeinde Wien*, Vienna, 1962. But the architectural history of the great projects has not yet been written. Some are in Werner Hegemann, *City Planning Housing*, 3 vols., New York, 1936–1938, while for Heinrich Schmid and Hermann Aichinger there is their own *Bauentwürfe von Wiener Architekten* (#6903b in the Rathaus archive), and for Karl Ehn, who was in charge of communal building for some of the most critical years and directed a large staff of architects and planners like that of the London County Council, there are his *Wohnhausbaubroschüren, 1926–36* (#36 in the archive).

75. On which see now: Otto Antonia Graf, *Die Vergessene Wagnerschule*, Vienna, 1969. It now seems evident to me that a definite influence is exerted by the work of Wagner, Olbrich, and the other Viennese on the work of Frank Lloyd Wright around 1900, and that the current runs in that direction rather than the reverse. However, there is direct influence from the American Shingle Style of the 80s, as from Wright, clearly apparent in some of the Viennese work toward 1904–05; as *Ibid*, figs. 105–108. English influence is also obvious. The whole problem needs renewed study by someone who knows both sides of the Atlantic and Central Europe better than any of us yet does.

76. One thinks here of Moore's Church Street South housing in New Haven, a noble attempt at urban amenities, bitterly criticized but not yet properly published.

77. Emile Aillaud, "Clefs pour Grigny," *L'Œil, 179* (November 1969), pp. 52–59; and also "La Grande Borne, Grigny," *Architecture d'Aujourd'hui, 144* (June, 1969), pp. 19–22. Now: Gérald Gassiot-Talabot and Alain Devy, *La Grande Borne à Grigny, Ville d'Emile Aillaud*, Paris, 1972. The lack of associated industries, of social services, and of proper transportation facilities constitutes, however, a serious deficiency in the design of "La Grande Borne."

78. Reyner Banham, *op. cit.*, pp. 116–117.

79. For Russian Constructivism as a whole see now Anatole Kopp, *Town and Revolution: Soviet Architecture and City Planning 1917–1935*, English trans. by Thomas E. Burton, New York, 1970; original edition *Ville et Revolution*, Paris, 1967. The book presents much documentary material. Other scholars are working on this supreme moment in Soviet art history, but the archival materials in terms of photographs and so on have so far generally turned out to be sadly elusive. Recent Soviet achievements in the industrialization of mass housing in precast concrete are

also impressive in a technical and methodological sense, and as a sustained attempt to solve an enormous housing problem. In general, the best discussion of contemporary Soviet architecture is found in *Architecture d'aujourd'hui*, December 1969–January 1970, no. 147. For a somewhat dated but more complete discussion of Soviet housing and the standardized use of prefabricated concrete panels, see *Casabella*, May 1962, no. 263.

80. *American Architecture and Urbanism*, pp. 144–154. Later, Stalin's skyscrapers owed as much to such New York monuments as the Woolworth Building and McKim, Mead, and White's Municipal Building as they did to the Kremlin's towers. For the Beaux-Arts skyscrapers also: Werner Hegemann (with Elbert Peets), *Amerikanische Architektur und Stadtbaukunst*, Berlin, 1925.

81. Reyner Banham, *op. cit.*, pp. 182–188.

82. George L. Hersey, *op. cit.*, p. 10. Again, my meaning is intended to be a simpler one. Few "associational" connections as for Hersey, and no "structural" ones as for Colquhon, Jencks, Baird, *et al.*, are involved in my use of the term. Form, sign, and/or symbol have always enjoyed a complex and constantly shifting interrelationship in human experience; and, having in mind E. H. Gombrich's remarkable preference for Soulages over Kline (*The Story of Art*, twelfth edition, London, 1972, pp. 479–480), I am not impressed by his award of the laurel for expression to symbol, often cited in this connection: E. H. Gombrich, *Meditations on a Hobby Horse and Other Essays on Art*, London and Greenwich, 1963, pp. 45–69. The relation of language to architecture, as Whorf analyzed it in Hopi culture, for example, is another matter: Benjamin Lee Whorf, "Linguistic Factors in the Terminology of Hopi Architecture," *International Journal of American Linguistics*, 19 (1953), pp. 141–145; reprinted in *Language, Thought, and Reality: Selected Writings of Benjamin Lee Whorf*, ed. with an introduction by John B. Carroll, Cambridge, Mass., 1956. I try to discuss Whorf's analysis in my "Men and Nature in Pueblo Architecture," in *American Indian Art: Form and Tradition*, Minneapolis, 1972, pp. 34–41. Also, my *Pueblo: Mountain Village Dance*, Chapter I. (Note 91 below).

83. See in general Barbara Rose, *Claes Oldenburg*, New York, 1970; and especially Barbara Haskell, *Claes Oldenburg, Object into Monument*, Pasadena, 1971, pp. 32–34.

84. Reyner Banham, *op. cit.*, pp. 191–192. James Stirling's History Faculty, for Cambridge University, designed later in the decade, should also be cited here for its constructivist connections. Still, in the boldness of his forms there and in buildings at Oxford and St. Andrews and in his exploitation of brick and glass, Stirling also remains, it seems to me, the liveliest embodiment of the great English nineteenth-century architectural tradition in a physical sense, while the Smithsons (leaving Archigram aside) have been its most systematic conceptualizers. The writings of the critic, Banham continue to be of interest in spite of some inaccurate digressions (*The Architecture of the Well-Tempered Environment*, 1969; *Los Angeles: The Architecture of Four Ecologies*, 1971).

85. The Technical College of Delft, by Van den Broek and Bakema, 1952–55.

These architects deserve more extended citation. Their Reformed Church at Nagele, Holland, of 1960, looks prototypical of Kahn's Rochester church and of some work by Peter Millard as well. See Banham, *op. cit.*, figs. 203–205.

86. *Archigram* is a lively publication which is supposed to appear yearly and more or less does so. Cf. Peter Cook, *Architecture: Action and Plan*, London, 1969, and *Experimental Architecture*, London, 1970; also Royston Landau, *New Directions in English Architecture*, New York, 1969.

87. For the Metabolists: *Architectural Design*, special issues of October, 1964; May, 1965; May, 1967, and: Robin Boyd, *New Directions in Japanese Architecture*, New York, 1969.

88. *American Architecture and Urbanism*, figs. 426, 427. All the recent cylinders of Japan and America alike should probably be referred back to an unbuilt project by Kahn: the Mikveh Israel Synagogue, of 1961–65. Also: John Jacobus, *Twentieth-Century Architecture: The Middle Years, 1940–1965*, New York, 1966; and Robert A. M. Stern, *New Directions in American Architecture*, New York, 1969.

89. *American Architecture and Urbanism*, pp. 225–226.

90. *Ibid.*, pp. 145 and 207; figs. 198, 199.

91. The spatial relation to the setbacks of Pueblo architecture is stressed by Safdie. My own interest in the pueblos dates from 1964 and is embodied in a book, *Pueblo: Mountain Village Dance*, scheduled for publication by Viking Press in 1974. This grows out of and contrasts with my work on Greek temples during what I have already described as modern architecture's heroically idealistic phase: *The Earth, the Temple, and the Gods. Greek Sacred Architecture*, New Haven, 1962; new enlarged edition New York, 1969.

92. Levi-Strauss, whose name has recently been so often and so portentously invoked by architectural critics that I hesitate to do so again, nevertheless once characterized the difference between the two periods as between the "dialectic" of Sartre and the "analysis" employed by himself: Claude Levi-Strauss, *The Savage Mind*, Chicago, 1966 (original edition *La Pensée Sauvage*, Paris, 1962), Chapter 9, "History and Dialectic," pp. 245–269 (cf. note 49, above). For America, the shift has had more emotional overtones, unavoidably present, I fear, in this book. Yet in this connection I cannot forebear citing the beautifully analyzed if undoubtedly sentimentalized essay by my friend, Charles Reich, in honor of whose hopes the piece from Wallace Stevens is (considering the subtitle, somewhat sardonically) quoted at the head of this section: Charles A. Reich, *The Greening of America*, New York, 1970.

93. This observation is the result of considerable research carried on in my seminar at Yale first by W. Perkins Foss and now by Jane Andrew, whose dissertation on the subject of mobile homes should be completed by 1974.

94. Jean Prouvé is an outstanding teacher and technician in light metal construction and industrial prefabrication in the strictest tradition of French structural determinism. Cf. Jean Prouvé, *Une Architecture par l'Industrie*, ed. by Benedikt Huber and Jean-Claude Steinegger, Zurich, 1971; English edition *Prefabrication: Structures and Elements*, trans.

by Alexander Lieven, New York, 1971. Prouvé will in a sense "design" only structural components; in this he represents the opposite pole of the French genius from that occupied by the great environmentalist, Emile Aillaud. Perhaps only in their Gothic cathedrals were the French ever able to bring the two utterly opposite obsessions wholly together. Le Corbusier is something else and stands alone as an analyzer of social programs and a master of forms. His genius—unlike that of Wright, which seems ever gentler and more directly personal in retrospect—is beginning to look more titanic with every passing year. His death and those of Wright and Mies leave gaps which will probably not be filled until some new era of human life is well underway.

95. An award winner for 1971: *Progressive Architecture*, January, 1972, pp. 64–65. Like all such winners, it is presumably slated for production.

96. Charles W. Moore, "Plug It In, Ramses, and See If It Lights Up," *Perspecta, 11*, 1967, pp. 34–43.

97. Robert Venturi, *et al., Learning From Las Vegas, op. cit.*, especially pp. 1–61.

98. As is usual these days, he avidly tells us (*Ibid.*, p. 169) all about those influences but not about how they came to his attention. Wright's normal procedure was to deny everything.

99. Cf. Michael Harrington, *The Other America: Poverty in the United States*, New York, 1962; and, *The Accidental Century*, New York, 1965; and *Socialism*, New York, 1970.

Numbers in regular roman type refer to text pages; *italic* figures refer to the plates.

Aalto, Alvar, 37, 38, 39, 40, 44, 55; Church, Vuoksenniska, *113–115*; Civic Center, Säynätsalo, 38, *117*, *118*; Housing, project, Munkkiniemi, 37, *116*

Acropolis, axis of the, with Horns of Hymettos, 41, *123*

"Across the Continent," *23*, 51

Adler & Sullivan (partnership), Guaranty Building, Buffalo, 19, 29, 53, 60, *32*; Wainwright building, St. Louis, 19, 53, *30*; Walker Warehouse, Chicago, 18–19, *29*. See also Sullivan, Louis

Aichinger (*See* Fuchsenfeldhof Houses)

Aillaud, Emile, 56; La Grande Borne, Grigny, 56, *167*

Airstream caravans, 61, *181*

All Saints Church, London (Butterfield), 16, 50, *20*

Alumni Memorial Hall, I.I.T. (Mies), *95*

American Architecture and Urbanism (Scully), 60

American colonial houses, 20, 21, *35a*, *36*, *37*

American frame construction, 21, *17*

American shingle style houses, 20, *34–35a*

Ames Gate Lodge, North Easton (Richardson), 18, *27*

Archigrams, 58–60

Art and Architecture Building, Yale University, New Haven, Conn. (Rudolph), 50, *153*

Art Nouveau, 22, 23, 31; German revolt against, 24

Ashurst House, Overbrook (Eyre), *34*

Assembly Building, Chandigarh (Le Corbusier), *146*

Auditorium, *Maison du Peuple*, Brussels (Horta), 22, 24, *45*

Bank of England, London (Soane), 12, 52, *4*

Barcelona Pavilion (Mies), 27, 28, *74–77*

Barnsdall House, Los Angeles (Wright), 29, *79*

Baroque, 11, 12, 14, 15, 16, 20, 22, *19–22*, 40. See also Beaux-Arts Baroque;

"Battle and Victory" Pageant design, Petrograd (Vesnin and Popova), 57, *172*

Bauhaus, Dessau (Gropius), 27, 33, 51, *68–70*

Beaux-Arts Baroque, 16, 29, 51, 57. See *also* Baroque

Behrens, Peter, Turbine Factory, Berlin, 25, 26, 27, 41, *56*

Berg, Max, 13, 23; Centennial Hall (Breslau), 13, 23, 52, *7*

Berlage, 41

Bismarck Monument, project for (Mies), 27

Boullée, 35

Brooklyn Bridge, New York (Roebling), 17, 51, *24*

Brown, Denise Scott (*See* Urban Center for Thousand Oaks)

Brunelleschi, 38

Burnham & Root (partnership), Reliance Building, Chicago, *31*

Butterfield, William, 15; All Saints Church, London, 16, 50, *20*

Café de Unie, Rotterdam (Oud), 26, *67*

Capital Buildings, Chandigarh, India (Le Corbusier), *144*

Capitol for East Pakistan, Dacca (Kahn), 52

Carceri etchings (Piranesi), 12, 52, *3*

Carson Pirie Scott Department Store, Chicago (Sullivan), 20, *33*

Casa Mila, Barcelona (Gaudí), 23, 54, *47*, *49*

Centennial Hall, Breslau (Berg), 13, 23, 52, *7*

Center City, Philadelphia, proposal (Kahn), 51, *156*

Centrosoyus, Moscow (Le Corbusier), 43, *130*

150

Chandigarh, India (*See* Le Corbusier)

Chicago School, architects of, 19, *31*

"Chicago" windows, 19, 20, *31*, *32*

Church at Vuoksenniska, Finland (Aalto) 37, *113–115*

Church Street South Public Housing, New Haven, Conn. (Moore), 55, *166*

Citrohan House, Weissenhof Housing Exhibition, Stuttgart (Le Corbusier), 42, *126*

City National Bank, Mason City, Iowa (Wright), 25–26, *60*

Civic Center, Säynätsalo, Finland (Aalto), 38, *117*, *118*

Club House of City Working Men's Union, Moscow (Melnikov), 58, *176*

Coliseum, New Haven, Conn. (Roche, Dinkeloo & Associates), 59, *178*

Colonial houses, American, 20, 21, *35a*, *36*, *37*

Colossal Monument proposal, Thames River (Oldenburg), 57, *174*

Commonwealth Apartments (Mies), 34

Community Center, Trenton. N.J. (Kahn), 38, *119*

Complexity and Contradiction in Architecture (Venturi), 53

"*Construction of Volume Relations*," (Vantongerloo), *64*

Constructivism, Russian, 56–59

Cook, Peter, 58; Project for a New University, Living City Exposition, London, 58, *177*

Cosmopolis of the Future, King's Dream of, New York, 57, *170*

Crystal Palace, London (Paxton), 12, 13, 52, *5*

Cubist painting, 22, 26

Cullinan Wing, Museum of Fine Arts, Houston, Texas (Mies), *103*

David, paintings by, 14, *10*

De Bretteville, Hodgetts and Kupper, 61; Design for a Mobile Theater, 61, *182*

De Klerk, Michel, 53–54; Post Office, Public Utility Housing, Amsterdam, 54, *162*

Deutsches Museum, Munich (Troost), 50, *152*

Dinkeloo (*See* Roche)

Dormitories, Bryn Mawr, Pa. (Kahn), 52

Dutert, Ferdinand (*See* Galerie des Machines)

Ecclesiological Gothic, 16, *20*

Ehn, Karl, 54; Heiligenstadt Houses, Karl Marx Hof, Vienna, 54, *163*

Eiffel Tower, 13

Einstein Tower, Neubabelsberg, Germany (Mendelsohn), 23, *50*

Engineering Laboratory, Leicester University, England (Stirling and Gowan), 58, *175*

Eyre, Wilson, Ashurst House, Overbrook, Pa., *34*

Fagus Factory, Alfeld-an-der-Leine (Gropius & Meyer), 25, *57*, *58*

"Falling Water," Kaufmann House, near Connellsville, Pa. (Wright), 30, *82*

Farnsworth House, Plano, Ill. (Mies), 34, *97*

Ferriss, Hugh 29

Fire Station #4, Columbus, Indiana (Venturi and Rauch), 61, *183*

Florida Southern College (Wright), 32

Folger (*See* House of Industry)

Frame construction, American, 21, *17*

Fuchsenfeldhof Houses, Vienna (Schmid and Aichinger), 55, *165*

Gabo, Naum, 27

Galerie des Machines, International Exposition, Paris (Dutert), 13, 52, *6*

Garage, Rue de Ponthieu, Paris (Perret), *51*

Garnier, Charles, L'Opéra, Paris, *22*

Gaudí, Antonio, 23, 54

Gemeindebauten, Vienna, 54

General Motors Research Center (Saarinen), 35

"Georgian", 16, *19–22*

German Pavilion, International Exposition, Barcelona (Mies), 27, 28, *74–77*

Gilbert, Cass, 57; Woolworth Building, New York, 57

Glass skyscraper, project for (Mies), 27, *71*

Goetsch-Winkler House, Okemos, Michigan (Wright), *83*

Gothic, Ecclesiological, 16; Revival theory, 17, 18, 33; Victorian, 15, 16

Government Center for New Haven, Conn., Redevelopment project, 50, *154*

Gowan (*See* Engineering Laboratory)

Graphic Arts Center project for Manhattan (Rudolph), 59

Greek architecture, 14, 35, 40, 41, 42, 44, *11, 13*

Gropius, Walter, 25, 26, 27, 30; Bauhaus, Dessau, 57, *68–70*; Fagus Factory, Alfeld-an-der-Leine, *57, 58*; Harvard University Graduate Center, Cambridge, Mass., 32, 33, *92*; Model Factory, Werkbund Exhibition, Cologne, *59, 61*

Guaranty Building, Buffalo (Adler & Sullivan), 19, 29, 34, 45, 53, 60, *32*

Guggenheim Museum, New York (Wright), 32, 37, *90, 91*

Guild House, Philadelphia, Pa. (Venturi and Rauch), 53–54, *160*

Habitat, Montreal (Safdie), 59, *180*

Hadrian's Villa, 32, 35; Serapieion at, 45; as related to Ronchamp (Le Corbusier), *138, 140*

Hameau, Le, Versailles (Mique & H. Robert), 15, *16*

Harris, Harwell Hamilton (*See* Johnson House), *18*

Harvard University Graduate Center, Cambridge, Mass. (Gropius), 32, 33, *92*

Heiligenstadt Houses, Karl Marx Hof, Vienna (Ehn), 54, *163*

High Court, Chandigarh, India, (Le Corbusier), 11, 12, 47, 48, 50, 52, *2, 144, 147–149, 151*

High School, Sarasota, Florida (Rudolph), 48, *150*

Hirschorn Museum, Washington, D.C., 50

Hodgetts (*See* Mobile Theater)

Ho-O-Den, 21

Horta, Victor, 22, 24; House Interior, Brussels, *44*; Maison du Peuple Auditorium, Brussels, *45*

Hôtel de Soubise, 22

House of German Art, Munich (Troost), 48, *152*

House of Industry, Kharkov, Soviet Union (Serafimov, Folger and Kravetz), 56, *169*

Illinois Institute of Technology (Mies), 33, 34, *93*

Indian Institute of Management, Ahmedabad (Kahn), 52, *159*

International Style, 26, 27, 30, 33, 37, 43, 55–56, 61

Izenour, Steven (*See* Urban Center for Thousand Oaks)

Japanese architecture, 21, 29

Jefferson, Thomas, 14, 17, *14*. *See* University of Virginia

Johnson House, Los Angeles (Harris), *18*

Johnson Library, Austin, Texas, 50

Johnson, Philip, 34, 35, 37; Kneses Tifereth Israel Synagogue, Portchester, N.Y., 35, *106–108*; Munson-Williams-Proctor Institute, Utica, N.Y., 35, *104*; Philip Johnson House, New Canaan, Conn., 35, *103a*; Seagram Building, New York (with Mies), 34, 53, 60, *100, 101*; Theater of the Dance, Lincoln Square, N.Y., 35, *105*

Johnson Wax Building, Racine, Wisconsin (Wright), 31, *87, 88*

Kahn, Louis I., 38–40, 44, 51–53, 55; Capitol for East Pakistan, Dacca, 52; Center City, Philadelphia, proposal, 51, *156*; Community Center, Trenton, N.J., *119*; Dormitories, Bryn Mawr, Pa., 52; Indian Institute of Management, Ahmedabad, 52, *159*; Jonas B. Salk Center for Biological Research, California, 52; Medical and Biology Laboratories, University of Pennsylvania, Philadelphia, 39, 51–52, *120–122*; Unitarian Church, Rochester, N.Y., 51, *157–158*; Yale Art Gallery, 38

Kaufmann House (*See* "Falling Water")

Kent House, Tuxedo Park, New York (Price), 61, *35, 35a*

Klenze, Leo von (*See* "Valhalla"

Kneses Tifereth Israel Synagogue, Portchester, N.Y. (Johnson), 35, 37, *106–108*

Knights of Columbus Building, New Haven, Conn. (Roche, Dinkeloo & Associates), 59, *178*

Kolbe, 28; sculpture for Barcelona Pavilion, *76*

Kravetz (*See* House of Industry)

Kresge Auditorium, M.I.T., Cambridge, Mass. (Saarinen), *109*

Kupper (*See* Mobile Theater)

La Grande Borne, Grigny (Aillaud), 56, *167*

Lakeshore Apartments, Chicago (Mies), 34, *98*

Larkin Building, Buffalo, N.Y. (Wright), 21, 39, *38, 39*

Le Corbusier, 11, 14, 39, 40, 41, 42, 43, 44–48, 50–53, 55–57, 60; Centrosoyus, Moscow, 43, *130*; Chandigarh, India: Assembly Building, *146*, Capital Buildings, *144*, High Court, 50, 52, *2, 147–149, 151*, Secretariat, *145*; Citrohan House, Weissenhof Housing Exhibition, Stuttgart, 42, *126*; Maisons Jaoul, Neuilly, 44, 52, 53, *132, 133*; Modulor, Le, 46, *142*; Monastery of La Tourette, Eveux, 46, 50, *143*; Notre Dame du Haut, Ronchamp, 45, *137–141*; Ozenfant House, Paris, 41, *125*; Palace of the Soviets, 43, 56, *128, 129*; Pavillon de l'Esprit Nouveau, 42; St. Dié, 47; Sarabhai Villa, Ahmedabad, 44; Swiss Dormitory, University City, Paris, 43, 56, *127*; Union of the Cooperatives, Moscow, 43, *130*; Unité d'Habitation, Marseilles, 44, 45, 53, 60, *134–136*; Villa Savoie, Poissy-sur-Seine, 14, *15*; "Ville Contemporaine," 41, 51, *124*; Ville Radieuse, 51, 56; Weekend House, Paris, suburbs of, *131*

Ledoux, Claude-Nicolas, 13, 14, 24, 35; house designs, 14, *13*; Salle de Spectacles, 14, *10*

Lenin Institute, model for project (Leonidov), 57, *173*

Leonidov, Ivan, Model of Project for Lenin Institute, 57, *173*

Lever House, New York (Skidmore, Owings & Merill), 34, *99*

Lincoln Center, New York, 50

Livestock Pavilion, Raleigh, N.C. (Nowicki & Dietrick), 13, 52, *8*

London County Council, 56; Roehampton Housing Development, Richmond Park, London, 56, *168*

Loos, Adolf, 24; Steiner House, Vienna, *55*

L'Opéra, Paris (Garnier), *22*

McGregor Memorial Conference Center, Wayne University, Detroit (Yamasaki, Leinsweber & Associates), 36, *111*

Maison du Peuple, Brussels, (Horta), 22, 24, *45*

Maisons Jaoul, Neuilly (Le Corbusier), 44, 52–53, *132, 133*

Marinetti, 57

Marshall Field Warehouse (Richardson), 18, *28*

Martin House, Buffalo, N.Y. (Wright), 21, *40*

Mason City National Bank, Mason City, Iowa (Wright), 25–26, *60*

Massachusetts Institute of Technology, Kresge Auditorium, Cambridge, Mass. (Saarinen), 35, 36, *109*

Medical & Biology Labs., University of Pennsylvania, Philadelphia (Kahn), 39, 51–52, *120–122*

Melnikov, 58; Club House of City Working Men's Union, Moscow, 58, *176*

Mendelsohn, Eric, Einstein Tower, 23, *50*

Meyer, Hannes (*See* Fagus Factory)

Mies van der Rohe, Ludwig, 27, 28, 30, 33, 34, 35, 36, 39, 42, 53, 60; Bismarck Monument, 27; brick country house, 27, *72, 73*; Commonwealth Apartments, 34; Cullinan Wing, Museum of Fine Arts, Houston, Texas, 35, *103*; Farnsworth House, Plano, Ill., 34, *97*; German Pavilion at Barcelona, 27, 28, *74–77*; Illinois Institute of Technology, 33, *93–95*; Lakeshore Apartments, Chicago, 34, *98*; National Theater, Mannheim, Germany, 34, *102*; Seagram Building, New York, (*with Philip Johnson*), 34, 53, 60, *100, 101*; skyscraper, glass, project for, 27, *71*; Tugendhat House, Brno, Czechoslovakia, 28, *78*

Mobile Homes, 59–60

Mobile Theater design (De Bretteville, Hodgetts and Kupper), 61, *182*

Model Factory, Werkbund Exhibition, Cologne (Gropius), 25, *59, 61*

Modulor, Le (Le Corbusier), 46, *142*

Monastery of La Tourette, Eveux (Le Corbusier), 46, 50, *143*

Mondriaan, 26

Moore, Charles, 55, 61; Church Street South Public Housing, New Haven, Conn., 55, *166*

Morris Gift Shop, San Francisco (Wright) 32, *89*

Munkkiniemi, Finland, housing project (Aalto), 37, *116*

Munson-Williams-Proctor Institute, Utica, N.Y. (Johnson), 35, *104*

Museum of Fine Arts, Houston, Texas (Mies), 35, *103*

153

National Farmers' Bank, Owatonna, Minn. (Sullivan), 53, *161*

National Theater, Mannheim, Germany (Mies), 34, *102*

Nervi, Pier Luigi, 13; Palazzetto dello Sport, 13, *9*

Neutra, Richard, 30

New Brutalism, 52-53, 59, *132, 136*

Newton, Dudley (See Sturtevant House)

New University project, Living City Exposition, London (Cook), 58, *177*

Notre Dame, Le Raincy (Perret), 24, *52*

Oak Street Connector, New Haven, Conn., 51, *155*

Octopus vase (Minoan), *46*

Oldenburg, Claes, 56–57; Proposed Colossal Monument, Thames River, 57, *174*

"Open Road" (*Walt Whitman's*), 17, 21, 30, *23*

Ostia Antica, 52

Oud, J. J. P., Café de Unie, Rotterdam, 26, *67*

Ozenfant House, Paris (Le Corbusier), 41, *125*

Palace of the Soviets (Le Corbusier), 43, 56, *128, 129*

Palazzetto dello Sport, Rome (Nervi & Vitellozzi), *9*

Pantheon, 13, *9*

Paris Opéra, 16

Park Hill Development, Sheffield, England (Sheffield City Architects Department), 57, *171*

Parson Capen House, Topsfield, Mass., *kitchen, 43*

Parthenon on Praeneste, 16, *19*

Pavillon Colbert, Louvre, Paris (Visconti & Lefuel), 21

Pavillon de l'Esprit Nouveau (Le Corbusier), 42

Paxton, John, 12, 13; Crystal Palace, London, 52, *5*

Perret, Auguste, 23, 24, 35, 41; garage, Rue de Ponthieu, Paris, *51*; Notre Dame, Le Raincy, *52*; Place de l'Hotel de Ville, Le Havre, 53

Pett, Tony (See Urban Center for Thousand Oaks)

Piranesi, Giovanni Battista, 12, 13, 16, 18, 43, 48, 52; Carceri series, *3*

Place de l'Hotel de Ville, Le Havre (Perret), 24, *53*

Plateau Beaubourg Project, Paris (Rogers, Piano, *et al.*), 58

Pop Art, 55–56

Popova, Lubov (See "Battle and Victory")

Post Office, Public Utility Housing, Amsterdam (De Klerk), 54, *162*

Post Office, Vienna (Wagner), 24, *54*

Price, Bruce; Kent House, Tuxedo Park, N.Y., 61, *35–35a*

Prouvé, Jean, 61

Rauch, John (See Venturi)

Redevelopment, American, 50–51, 53–54, 62

Reichs Congress Hall, Nuremberg (Ludwig & Franz Ruff), 14, *11*

Reliance Building, Chicago (Burnham & Root), *31*

Renaissance architecture, 16, 18, 33, 45

Reumann, Jakob, 54

"Rhythm of a Russian Dance," (Van Doesburg), *63*

Richards Medical Research Building, University of Pennsylvania, Philadelphia (Kahn), 39, *120–122*

Richardson, Henry Hobson, 18, 19, 20, 21, 25, 32; Ames Gate Lodge, North Easton, Mass., 18, *27*; Marshall Field Warehouse, Chicago, 18, *28*; Parson Capen House *(kitchen), 43*; Stoughton House, Cambridge, Mass., *26*; Watts-Sherman House, Newport, R.I., 18, *25*

Rietveld, Gerrit, 26; Project for a private house *(with* Van Doesburg), *65*; Shröder House, Utrecht, *66*

Robert, Mique & H. (See Le Hameau)

Robie House, Chicago (Wright), 21–22, 41, *42*

Roche, Dinkeloo & Associates, 59; Coliseum and Knights of Colombus Building, New Haven, Conn., 59, *178*

Roebling, John Augustus (See Brooklyn Bridge)

Roehampton Housing Development, Richmond Park, London (London County Council), 56, *168*

Rogers, Piano, *et al.*, Plateau Beaubourg Project, Paris, 58

Ronchamp (Notre Dame du Haut) (Le Corbusier), 45, 46, *137–141*

154

Rotival, Maurice, 51; Oak Street Connector, New Haven, Conn., 51, *155*

Rudolph, Paul, 50, 59; Art and Architecture Building, Yale University, New Haven, Conn., 50, *153*; Graphic Arts Center project for Manhattan, 59; High School, Sarasota, Florida, 48, *150*

Ruscha, Edward, 55

Saarinen, Eero, 35, 36; General Motors Research Center, 35; Kresge Auditorium, M.I.T., Cambridge, Mass., 35, 36, *109*

Safdie, Moshe, 59; Habitat, Montreal, 59, *180*

St. Dié (Le Corbusier), 47

St. Mark's Tower project, New York (Wright), 29, *80*

Salk Center for Biological Research, California (Kahn), 52

Salle de Spectacles (Ledoux), 14, *10*

Sant'Elia, 57

Sarabhai Villa, Ahmedabad (Le Corbusier), 44

Säynätsalo Civic Center, Finland (Aalto), 38, *117, 118*

Schmid and Aichinger, Fuchsenfeldhof Houses, Vienna, 55, *165*

Scott, Geoffrey, 19, 45

Seagram Building, New York (Mies & Johnson), 34, 53, 60, *100, 101*

Secondary School, Hunstanton, England (Smithson, Peter & Alison), 33, 39, *96*

Secretariat, Chandigarh, India (Le Corbusier), 47, *145*

Seitz, Karl, 54

Serafimov, Folger and Kravetz, House of Industry, Kharkov, Soviet Union, 56, *169*

Shingle Style houses, American, 20, 61, *34–35a*

Shröder House, Utrecht, (Rietveld), 66

Sitte, Camillo, 55

Skidmore, Owings & Merrill, 34, 36; Lever House, New York, *99*; U.S. Air Force Academy, Colorado Springs, *112*

Skyscraper, glass, project for (Mies), 27, *71*

Smithson, Peter & Alison, 57, Secondary School, Hunstanton, England, 33, 39, *96*

Soane, Sir John, 12, 13; Bank of England, 52, *4*

Spanish Stairs, Rome (Specchi and De Sanctis), 11, 12, *1*

"Starry Night" (Van Gogh), *48*

Steiner House, Vienna (Loos), 55

"Stick Style" houses, 15, 18, *17*

Stijl, de, 26, 33

Stirling, James, 39, 44

Stirling and Gowan, 58; Engineering Laboratory, Leicester University, England, 58, *175*

Stone, Edward, 36; U.S. Embassy, New Delhi, India, *110*

Stoughton House, Cambridge, Mass. (Richardson), *26*

Stuart and Revett, 14; Tower of the Winds, *12*

Sturtevant House, Middletown, R.I. (Newton), 15, *17*

Sullivan, Louis, 18, 19, 21, 22, 25, 29, 34, 40, 53, 57, 60; Carson-Pirie-Scott Department Store, 20, *33*; National Farmers' Bank, Owatonna, Minnesota 57, *161*. *(See* also Adler and Sullivan)

Swiss Dormitory, University City, Paris (Le Corbusier), 43, 56, *127*

Taliesin West, Phoenix, Arizona (Wright), 30–31, *84–86*

Tange, Kenzo, 59; Yamanashi Communications Center, Kofu, Japan, 59, *179*

Theater of the Dance, Lincoln Square, N.Y. (Johnson), 35, *105*

Tower of the Winds (Stuart and Revett), 14, *12*

Trajan's Market, Rome, 52

Troost, P. L., 48; Deutsches Museum, Munich, 50, *152*

Trubek and Wislocki Houses, Nantucket, Mass. (Venturi, Rauch and Vaughan), 61, *184*

Tugendhat House, Brno, Czechoslovakia (Mies), 28, *78*

Turbine Factory, Berlin (Behrens), 25, *56*

Union of the Cooperatives, Moscow (Le Corbusier), 43, *130*

Unitarian Church, Rochester, N.Y. (Kahn), 51, *157–158*

Unité d'Habitation, Marseilles (Le Corbusier), 44, 45, 53, 60, *134–136*

United States Air Force Academy, Colorado Springs (Skidmore, Owings & Merrill), 36, *112*

United States Embassy, New Delhi, India (Stone), *110*

University of Virginia, Charlottesville, Va., 14, *14*

Urban Center for Thousand Oaks, California (Venturi *with* Izenour, Pett, and Brown), 55, *164*

"Usonian" houses (Wright), 30

"Valhalla," Regensburg (von Klenze), 16, *19*

Van Doesburg, Theo, 26, 27; Project for a private house *(with Rietveld), 65*; "Rhythm of a Russian Dance," *63*

Van Gogh, Vincent *("Starry Night")*, 23, *48*

Vantongerloo, George, 26; "Construction of Volume Relations," *64*

Vaughan, Terry *(See* Trubek and Wislocki Houses)

Venturi, Robert, 52–53, 55–56, 58–59, 61; *Complexity and Contradiction in Architecture*, 53; Fire Station #4, Columbus, Indiana *(with* Rauch), 61, *183*; Guild House, Philadelphia, Pa. *(with* Rauch), 53–54, *160*; Trubek and Wislocki Houses, Nantucket, Mass. *(with* Rauch and Vaughan), 61, *184*; Urban Center for Thousand Oaks, California *(with* Izenour, Pett, and Brown), 55, *164*

"*Vers une Architecture*," (Le Corbusier) 41

Vesnin, Alexander, 57; "Battle and Victory" Pageant design, Petrograd *(with* Popova), 57, *172*

Villa Savoie, Poissy-sur-Seine (Le Corbusier), 14, *15*

"*Ville Contemporaine, Une*" (Le Corbusier), 41, 51, *124*

Ville Radieuse (Le Corbusier), 51, 56

Viollet-le-Duc, 16, 24

Visconti & Lefuel, Pavillon Colbert, Louvre, Paris, *21*

Vitellozzi, A *(See* Palazzetto dello Sport)

Vuoksenniska Church, Finland (Aalto), 37, *113–115*

Wagner, Otto, 24, 54; Post Office, Vienna, *54*

Wainwright Building, St. Louis, Mo. (Adler & Sullivan), 19, 53, *30*

Walker Warehouse, Chicago (Adler & Sullivan), 18–19, *29*

Watts-Sherman House, Newport, R.I. (Richardson), 18, *25*

Wayne University *(See* McGregor Memorial Conference Center)

Weissenhof Housing Exhibition, Stuttgart, 42, *126*

Whitman, Walt, 17, 21

Willitts, Ward House, Highland Park, Ill. (Wright), 26, *36, 37, 62*

Wilson, Colin, 39

Woolworth Building, New York (Gilbert), 57

Wright, Frank Lloyd, 20, 21, 22, 25, 26, 27 28, 29, 30, 31, 32, 37, 39, 42, 43, 44, 46; Barnsdall House, Los Angeles, *79*; "Broadacre City," 30; City National Bank, Mason City, Iowa, 25–26, *60*; "Falling Water," Kaufmann House, 30, *82*; Florida Southern College, 32; Goetsch-Winkler House, Okemos, Mich., *83*; Guggenheim Museum, N.Y., *90, 91*; Johnson Wax Building, Racine, Wis., 31, *87, 88*; Larkin Building, Buffalo, N.Y., 21, *38, 39*; Martin House, Buffalo, N.Y., 21, *40*; Morris Store, San Francisco, 32, *89*; Robie House, Chicago, 21–22, *41, 42*; St. Mark's Tower project, N.Y., 29, *80*; Taliesin West, Phoenix, Arizona 30–31, *84–86*; "Usonian" houses, 30; Ward Willitts House, Highland Park, Ill., *36, 37, 62*; Yahara Boat Club Project, 26

Yahara Boat Club Project (Wright), 26

Yale Art Gallery (Kahn), 38

Yamanashi Communications Center, Kofu, Japan (Tange), 59, *179*

Yamasaki, Leinweber & Associates, McGregor Memorial Conference Center, Wayne University, Detroit, 36, *111*

SOURCES OF ILLUSTRATIONS

ABC, 2nd series, no. 1, Basel, 1926: 172

Wayne Andrews, New York: 16, 18, 27, 36, 42, 79

Archigram Architects, © Peter Cook: 177

The Architect and Building News, photo Sydney W. Newbery: 20

Architectural Design, photo John Donat: 175

Architectural Forum, Jan. 1938: 80

Architectural Review, photo de Burgh Galwey: 96, 168; photo Rayner Banham: 171

Archivos Amigos de Gaudi, Barcelona: 47

T. B. Bennett, *Architectural Design in Concrete* (New York, 1927): 7

Roy Barnard Co., Inc., New York: 50

Courtesy de Bretteville, Hodget and Kupper: 182

Courtesy Brooklyn Museum, New York: 46

Canadian Government Travel Bureau Photo: 180

Louis Checkman, Jersey City, New Jersey: 110

Chevojon, Paris: 6, 53

Chicago Architectural Photo Company, Chicago, Illinois: 28, 29, 31, 32, 33

W. K. Covell, Newport, Rhode Island: 17

Ralph Crane: 181

George Cserna, New York: 90, 91, 122

Robert Damora, New York: 92

Downing and Scully, *Architectural Heritage of Newport, Rhode Island* (Cambridge, Massachusetts, 1952): 25

John Ebstel, New York: 121, 157, 158

Bill Engdahl, Hedrich-Blessing, Chicago, Illinois: 41, 95, 103

Fairchild Aerial Surveys, New York: 81

Foto Mas, Barcelona: 49

Reimar F. Frank, Milwaukee, Wisconsin: 87, 88

General Electric Company, Cleveland, Ohio: 108

Alexandre Georges, New City, New York: 106

Walter Gropius, Cambridge, Massachusetts: 57, 58, 59, 61, 68, 69, 70 (photo Lucia Moholy)

Peter E. Guerrero, New York: 84, 86

Frederick Gutheim, Washington, D.C.: 114, 117

Heikki Havas, Helsinki, Finland: 115

Bill Hedrich, Hedrich-Blessing, Chicago, Illinois: 30, 82, 102, 112

Hedrich-Blessing, Chicago, Illinois: 97

Lucien Hervé, Paris: 126, 127, 128, 129, 130, 132, 133, 136, 138, 139, 140, 141, 145, 147, 149

Arthur M. Hind, *Giovanni Battista Piranesi* (New York, 1922): 3

David Hirsch, New York: 183

Henry-Russell Hitchcock, Jr., Northampton, Massachusetts: 60, 67, 143

Illustrated London News, July 21, 1956: 151

Steve Izenour, Philadelphia: 184

Courtesy Sidney Janis Gallery, New York: 174

Japan Architect, photo Osamu Murai: 179

Philip Johnson, New York: 105, 107

Louis I. Kahn, Philadelphia, Pennsylvania: 119, 120, 156, 159

G. E. Kidder Smith, New York: 52, 135

In A. Kopp, *Town and Revolution*, New York, 1970: 173

Baltazar Korab, Birmingham, Michigan: 111

Laboratorio Fotografico, Rome: 9

W. A. Lambeth and W. H. Manning, *Thomas Jefferson as an Architect* (Cambridge, Massachusetts, 1913): 14

L'Architecture Vivante, Spring-Summer: 1931: 15

Photo Standish Lawder, Yale University: 172

Le Corbusier, *L'Œuvre Complète* (Zurich, 1910–57), Vol. 1: 124, 125; Vol. 3: 131; Vol. 5: 2; Vol. 6: 137, 144, 146

Lever House, New York: 99

Photo Neil Levine, Yale University: 167, 178

London County Council: 168

Rollie McKenna, New York: 101

Joseph W. Molitor, Ossining, New York: 8

S. Moreux, *Claude-Nicolas Ledoux, Les Architectures Françaises* (Paris, 1945): 10

Museum of Modern Art, New York: 26, 38, 39, 44, 51, 54, 56, 63, 64, 65, 66, 71, 72, 73, 77, 78, 83, 85, 93, 116, 134; Lillie P. Bliss Bequest: 48

Museum of the City of New York; The Harry T. Peters Collection: 23

National Buildings Record, London: 4

New England Society of Antiquities, Cambridge, Massachusetts: 43

Maynard L. Parker, Los Angeles, California: 89

Photo Juji Noga, New Haven, Connecticut: 153

Courtesy Kevin Roche, John Dinkeloo, and Associates, Hamden, Connecticut: 178

Sharon Ryder, New York: 166

A. A. Schechter Associates, New York: 100

Ernst Scheidegger, Zurich: 148

Courtesy Vincent Scully, Jr., New Haven, Connecticut: 123

G. W. Sheldon, *Artistic Country Seats* (New York, 1886–87): 34, 35, 35a

Skomark Associates, New Jersey: 160

Smithsonian Institution, Washington. D.C.: 118

I. Steinman, *The Builders of the Bridge* (New York, 1945): 24

George Steuer, Oconomowoc, Wisconsin: 98

Franz Stoedtner, Düsseldorf: 19, 176

Ezra Stoller, Rye, New York, 99 100, 103a, 104, 109

Stuart and Revett, *Antiquities of Athens* (London, 1762): 12

Sovfoto, New York: 169

Photo Neil Thompson, courtesy Louis I. Kahn, Philadelphia: 159

P. L. Troost, *Das Bauen im Neuen Reich* (Bayreuth, 1938): 11, 52

Venturi and Rauch, Philadelphia: 164

Verlag von Anton Schroll and Co., Vienna: 55

Verlag Wasmuth, *Ausgeführte Bauten und Entwürfe von Frank Lloyd Wright* (Berlin 1910): 37; C. R. Ashbee, *Frank Lloyd Wright: Ausgeführte Bauten* (Berlin, 1911): 40, 62

Leonard von Matt, Buochs, Switzerland: 1

Courtesy Ware Library, Columbia University, New York: 21, 22

Williams and Meyer, Chicago, Illinois: 75

Courtesy Yale University Art Library, New Haven, Connecticut: 5, 13, 142, 150, 151, 154–155, 161–163, 165, 170

Zodiac, III: 113